DEB

Geographer, Scientist, Antarctic Explorer

D1388441

For all our widely travelled family

DEB
Geographer, Scientist, Antarctic Explorer

A biography of Frank Debenham, OBE, MA (Cantab), D.SC.HON. (Perth, Durham,
Sydney), The Polar Medal, Emeritus Professor of Geography
in the University of Cambridge

PETER SPEAK

PUBLISHING

in association with the

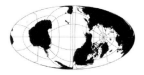

Scott Polar Research Institute
University of Cambridge

Published by
Polar Publishing Limited
10 Meadow Road
Burpham
Guildford
Surrey GU4 7LW

in association with
Scott Polar Research Institute
University of Cambridge
Lensfield Road
Cambridge CB2 1ER

Peter Speak has asserted his right under the Copyright, Designs and
Patents Act 1998 to be identified as the author of this work.

A catalogue record for this book is available from the British Library.

ISBN: 978-0-9548003-1-4   ISBN: 978-0-9548003-2-1 (hbk)

Page design and typesetting by Wileman Design, Farnham, Surrey
Printed and bound in Great Britain by TJ International, Padstow, Cornwall

Contents

Illustrations and Maps

Colour plates:

Foreword

The Scott Polar Research Institute, a part of the University of Cambridge, was founded in 1920 as the nation's memorial to Capt. R.F. Scott and his four companions who died on their return journey from the South Pole in 1912.

Quite simply, the Institute would not have come into existence without the vision and tenacity of Frank Debenham, who became its first Director in 1920 and was also Professor of Geography in Cambridge. It was Deb's proposal to the Trustees of the Scott Memorial Fund that suggested the establishment of a polar research centre, and that it should be located in Cambridge. Debenham had been a scientific member of Scott's *Terra Nova* Expedition, working as a geologist. He was very conscious that science as well as exploration was a strong theme on both of Scott's Antarctic expeditions, having assimilated the array of scientific achievements set out in the 14 volumes of reports from Scott's first, *Discovery* Expedition. It was that legacy of scientific achievement and experience in exploration that Debenham strove to perpetuate through the Scott Polar Research Institute. Debenham oversaw the design and construction of the now Grade-II listed 1934 building, which makes up about one-third of the present Institute's home in Cambridge, retiring from the Directorship only after World War II.

Since that time, the Institute has grown to house more than 50 staff, including academics undertaking research and teaching in the University, over 20 doctoral and masters students, and a support staff including those responsible for the library, archives and museum. The library is the pre-eminent polar collection world-wide, and the archives and museum safeguard and display works of art, artefacts, diaries and documents that span the whole period of exploration, especially British exploration, of the polar regions. The remit of the Institute includes both the Arctic and Antarctic and the physical and social sciences, with investigations of glaciers, ice sheets and their past, present and likely future responses to environmental change being a key focus. The Institute is supported by a Friends organisation, which celebrated its own 60th Anniversary earlier this year. Members of the Debenham family continue to be involved in the activities of the Institute through the Friends, providing a valued link back to Deb's own vital contributions.

Peter Speak's book is the first to focus on the life and achievements of Frank Debenham. It draws out the man and the historical context in which he lived and worked. It is also proves to be a very effective history of the Scott Polar Research Institute, its foundation in memory of Scott, Bowers, Evans, Oates and Wilson, and its subsequent development into a major international centre for polar research and information that I hope both Debenham and Scott, with their strong commitment to science, would have approved of.

PROFESSOR JULIAN DOWDESWELL
Director, Scott Polar Research Institute
November 2006

Acknowledgements

A great advantage of compiling a biography of a person only relatively recently deceased is the number of family, friends, colleagues and former students, who have still a good recall of that person's life, achievements and personality. I have been able to draw quite freely on these memories: sometimes it was only a passing reference, at others I was given a detailed account of Deb's life. Not all of these can I now acknowledge – for some I have even forgotten the attribution myself. I am, however, pleased to give thanks to the following and hope that if I have omitted anyone I may be forgiven.

Happily five of Deb's six children are still alive, though some a long distance from Cambridge. I was delighted to spend time with Deb's two daughters, Barbara and June, and thank them for their recollections of their father; I am also pleased to acknowledge help from his granddaughter, Philippa Foster Back, who supplied a number of photographs of Deb at an early age and of his family life. Elizabeth Peake (Rought) was the last of Deb's 'gels', who acted as Assistant to the Director; she filled in the details of the years at the end of the war and until Deb retired, and gave me copies of important correspondence from those days. Ann Shirley (Savours), who spent a number of years in the 1950s as guest in the family household, proved an excellent sounding board for many ideas.

I am particularly grateful to John Heap, recent Director of the Institute, who spent a morning of reminiscence about Deb with me only the week before he died in March 2006.

The records of the Scott Polar Research Institute were the springboard for the main outline of Deb's work in Cambridge. I am grateful for the access to manuscripts and personal diaries held in the Institute's archives prepared for me by the Archivist, Naomi Boneham, and for ever-ready help from the Librarian, Heather Lane, and her assistant Shirley Sawtell. A special word of thanks goes to the Photographic Librarian, Lucy Martin who sorted through the hundreds of negatives and prints to provide pictures of Deb.

At the Royal Geographical Society important documents were located by the Archivist Officer, Sarah Strong.

Special thanks are due to Harry King, for many years Librarian of the Institute. He has been a mine of information, recalling much by anecdote, and keeping my research focussed along the right paths. He has proofread all the manuscript and given very sound advice. Shirley Wittering has helped considerably in sorting out my desktop PC, and has taken many of the new digital photographs for the book.

I am indebted to Heather Lane, Librarian, and to Julian Dowdeswell, Director of the Institute, for their encouragement and for arranging the process of publishing the manuscript. In this context I am particularly grateful to Solveig Gardner Servian of Polar Publishing Ltd for her meticulous editing skills and for many suggestions that I have been pleased to incorporate in the book.

I should like also to mention Professor Emeritus Peter Friend of the Department of Earth Sciences, Professor Emeritus Alan Baker of the Cambridge Department of Geography, and David Stoddart, Professor Emeritus of Berkeley University, California, for their interest and specialised knowledge of Deb's work within the University of Cambridge.

Acknowledgment is also gratefully recognised of a paper by Peter Bryan and Nick Wise, published in the Proceedings of the Cambridge Antiquarian Society (2005, XCIV, 205, 199–216) on *Cambridge New Town – A Victorian Microcosm*, which outlined in detail the development of the southern fringe of Cambridge after the Enclosure Act of 1811 that ultimately made available the site on which the present Scott Institute of Polar Research now stands.

Sources of illustrations are given with the relevant picture or map. I am grateful for being able to reproduce plans of the site of the Institute from the *University Reporter*, by kind permission of the Chancellor, Master and Scholars of the University of Cambridge.

SPRI pictures are reproduced by permission of the Director, Professor Julian Dowdeswell. They include a photograph by Charles Swithinbank (statue, P2003/8/4). Other donors of photographs, namely Julian Inglas (P79/28) and Colin Vickridge (P200/85/1), I have been unable to trace, and I trust they will accept this as recognition. Other photographs, without attribution, have been taken by myself.

Introduction

When I first came up to Cambridge in 1946 to read for a Degree in Geography, the name of the Professor, Frank Debenham, meant nothing to me. Of course I recognised Capt. Scott, Wilson, Bowers, Oates and Evans who carried the major roles in the British Antarctic Expedition (1910–13) and were to perish on the return journey from the South Pole. But this had been a large expedition and most of the supporting members occupied the small print of the official record. As soon as I discovered that Deb (as he was known, familiarly, in Cambridge) had been with Scott on this famous Antarctic expedition, and when I met him, I was instantly captivated by his personality. Here was someone who had been to the southernmost end of the earth. In those days every candidate for a geography degree had an inborn curiosity about exotic places and the desire to be an explorer; Deb knew this, and he illuminated his lectures by anecdotal references to his own travels.

Many have commented on the avuncular nature of Deb: very approachable, always available to listen and encourage, and to dispense advice in a cheerful manner. John Heap, a former Director of the Scott Polar Research Institute, summed up Deb's personality as 'a people's person'. His monumental contribution to Cambridge academia comprise the Department of Geography, where he was the first Professor and the principal architect of the new building, and the Scott Polar Research Institute (SPRI, or 'the Institute'), where he was the Founder and first Director. In both centres of learning, Deb was insistent on presenting an environment where study could take place in an atmosphere of good fellowship surrounded by works of art as well as science. His buildings were designed to welcome visitors from afar as well as from Britain, and to encourage comradeship. He always hoped that young men and women would come to these centres of learning to practise their geography by organising expeditions, particularly to the polar regions and to mountainous terrain.

Deb was born in Bowral, in the hills of New South Wales, Australia, and attended a senior school in Parramatta in the northern suburbs of Sydney. He entered the University of Sydney in 1902 to read first for a degree in English and classics, and then moved to teach in a boys' boarding school in Armidale for some three years. In 1908 he returned to the University for a complete change – to study for a degree in geology, specialising in petrology. The Professor of Geology was Tannant William Edgeworth David, a Welshman by birth, who had studied in Oxford before taking this post in Australia. He had accompanied Shackleton in *Nimrod*, on the British Antarctic Expedition (1907–1909), and when Scott arrived in Sydney on his way to Antarctica he made a courtesy call to Edgeworth David and asked him to recommend a young Australian geologist to join *Terra Nova*. Deb was put forward even though he was a very recent graduate in the subject and had no experience of the kind of terrain he would meet in the Antarctic. Deb could not believe his good fortune, and many years later could scarcely understand how Scott had made this choice, for Scott had already appointed two other geologists with experience of working on ice sheets and amongst glaciers. It was to prove the most significant moment of Deb's life; his professional career veered to the extreme South, and when the expedition was over it seemed inevitable that he should follow his new-found friends to England, and particularly to Cambridge University where lay their ambitions to fulfil the rest of their days. Deb arrived in Cambridge in 1913 and was destined never to leave it. The remainder of his life was to be devoted to providing a memorial to Capt. Scott and his doomed colleagues, and to make a meaningful academic life, not in geology, his preferred subject, but in its sister discipline, geography.

For myself, on graduation I was determined to stay in Cambridge if this would prove possible. I was appointed to teach geography at the Cambridgeshire College of Arts and Technology in Cambridge (now Anglia Ruskin University), and eventually became Head of the Geography Department. It allowed me to keep in touch with the many staff and curriculum changes in the University, and to use the facilities of SPRI. I remember attending a Saturday evening lecture given by Deb, then in retirement, on the Scott Expedition; such was the demand for the meeting that the venue was moved from SPRI's museum to the Perse Boys School in Hills Road. When the opportunity arose for a sabbatical year it was only natural that I should turn to SPRI, and I joined the new course for the Master of Philosophy in Polar Studies in 1981–82. A few years later I resigned from my college appointment to continue research at SPRI. After a further two years I was asked to direct the M.Phil. course at the Institute, and managed this course for five years. Since then I have continued my close attachment to SPRI as Senior Research Associate, and have served on the committee of The Friends of SPRI. Deb's aim of creating a polar club at SPRI has obviously been successful, for at any time there will be former members of staff, many now long-time retired, both from SPRI and from the British Antarctic Survey, recalling their own expeditions to the Arctic or Antarctic, using the library's reading rooms, and acting as advisors to new generations of polar scholars.

I was delighted to take up the suggestion by many members of SPRI of writing this biography, and very pleased to have the agreement of the present Director, Professor Julian Dowdeswell, who encouraged me throughout and has contributed the Foreword. For me it has been a real pleasure.

PETER SPEAK
Cambridge, 2006

CHAPTER 1
Australia to Cambridge via Antarctica

Frank Debenham – Deb to friends and colleagues – was born on 26 December 1883 at Bowral, a small upcountry town some 2,000 ft (609 m) above sea level in the hills of New South Wales, Australia. He died at the age of 81 in Cambridge, England, on 23 November 1965.

Deb is remembered as an important Antarctic explorer, a fine academic geographer and an excellent administrator. His principal memorials are a mountain, a group of islands and a glacier named after him in Antarctica, and two significant buildings in Cambridge – the Department of Geography and the Scott Polar Research Institute (SPRI, or 'the Institute'). There are many friends and former students who have good reason to be grateful to him for his inspiration in geography and polar studies, and for the elegant buildings and resources he provided for them in Cambridge. In an address delivered at Debenham's memorial service, Lord McNair said that he:

> 'Was one of the most modest and unself-regarding persons that I have ever known. He was a good organiser and knew how to get the best out of those working with him, mainly because he was generous in giving credit to others and because he inspired their affection and confidence.'

The memorial service for Frank Debenham was held in the chapel of his old college Gonville and Caius in Cambridge, and conducted by the College Dean, Rev. J.V.M. Sturdy on Wednesday, 1 December 1965. Apart from the immediate members of his family, the University was represented by the great and good of academia, including Lord Adrian of Trinity, Professor Sir Neville Mott, Head of the Cavendish Laboratory and Master of Gonville and Caius, and the Masters of Magdalene, Pembroke and St Catherine's Colleges. The Department of Geography was represented by Professor H.C. Darby and lecturer W.W. Williams together with Mr and Mrs A.T. Grove (a lecturer in Geography and his wife, a former research student, Jean Clark). The Scott Polar Research Institute was represented by the Director, Dr Gordon de Quetteville Robin, and past Director, Dr Colin Bertram. Other eminent scholars included Dr Geoffrey Bushnell, anthropologist, Dr Joseph Needham, expert on the history of science in China, and Brian Harland, geologist, whose special interest was in the Svalbard archipelago of the Arctic. The British Antarctic Survey was represented by Dr Charles Swithinbank, and Arctic explorers by Lt Quintin Riley. Sadly, neither Raymond Priestley nor any surviving member of Scott's *Terra Nova* Expedition appear to have been present; most were, by this time, deceased.

In the memorial readings the Dean included an appropriate passage from Job 28; 12–28:

> Where shall wisdom be found?
> And where is the place of understanding?
> God understands the way to it,
> and he knows its place.
> For he looks to the ends of the earth,
> and sees everything under the heavens.

Deb sought understanding through his abiding interest in landscape, be it in his early geological studies, his awakening to the landscapes of ice in Antarctica during Scott's expedition, or in his later hydrological surveys of parts of southern Africa. He had travelled to one end of the earth and encouraged many others, particularly the Oxford and Cambridge University Mountaineering and Explorers' Clubs, to seek the other end, the Arctic.

Gordon Manley was a student of Deb's in the 1930s. He went on to become Professor of Geography at Bedford College, University of London, and an expert on Britain's climate, returning to Cambridge for his retirement. He also gave a series of lectures on meteorology and climate in the Department of Geography after the Second World War. Manley wrote in his obituary of Deb:

> 'He was a man of exceptional breadth of accomplishment. He will be
> mourned not only by the multitude of those who, at one time or
> another, were among his students, whether as undergraduates, as service
> cadets or as Colonial probationers; but also by a wide circle of friends,
> explorers and fellow scientists who knew of his achievements and the
> lively warmth of his personality.'

During the war Deb had created a short course for young service personnel in the art of navigation, and after the war he advised and helped direct the Cambridge course for those intending to enter the Colonial Service. Throughout his professional life, Deb was absorbed with the cartographical skills and practical difficulties of map-making and the complexities of astro-navigation. He had honed his survey skills in Antarctica on Scott's British Antarctic Expedition 1910–13, and was chosen to become the official author of the *Report on Maps and Survey* published in 1923. Manley recalled the early days of the Department of Geography:

'in the attics of the Sedgwick Museum where we learnt the art of survey surrounded by Antarctic equipment, and enjoyed some remarkable privileges. There was the day when one re-worked from the original sheet, that beautifully figured set of latitude sights taken by Bowers at the South Pole.'

Deb's maps were still in use during the International Geophysical Year 1957–58, according to Gordon de Q. Robin, the Director of SPRI between 1958 and 1982.

Debenham's first post at Cambridge was in 1919 as the Royal Geographical Society's lecturer in surveying and cartography, which he held in the embryonic Department of Geography. According to Robin, Deb:

'was the most good-hearted of men and the most receptive of listeners, modest but firm in his opinions, and never too busy to turn all his energies to the solution of some-one else's problems.'

Another Antarctic explorer of the 1930s, and former Director of SPRI (1949–56), Dr Colin Bertram wrote of Deb:

'His was a life of vigour and indeed vision, for he constantly looked ahead to new organisations and new methods which should be improvements on those already in being. Into old age he retained his enthusiasms, his friendships and his continued interest and writing on a variety of practical topics in the realms of cartography and survey.'

James Alfred Steers, who graduated with a first-class degree in Geography in 1921, was associated with Deb for most of Deb's time in Cambridge, from 1919 to 1965. As an undergraduate Steers was devoted to the subject, specialising in physical geography, and later was appointed as lecturer in the subject in the Department; he succeeded Deb in 1946 as Professor of Geography. In a tribute to Deb he wrote:

'He was essentially a practical man; he encouraged scholarship and was an excellent organiser. His happy personality made itself felt outside the Department and, with Priestley, Wordie and others, was a promoter of many Polar and other expeditions from Cambridge between the two wars. He will long be remembered as a good friend and as one who encouraged any who sought his help and advice to go out into the field and learn, as every geographer should, on the ground.'

This same sentiment was repeated by Brian Roberts, a former student of Deb's in the early 1930s, and one of those who attended Debenham's Easter camps of the Geographical Club at Austwick in Yorkshire and Patterdale in the Lake District:

'He was always approachable by everyone, however junior, and he was always a source of encouragement and inspiration to young people who wanted to become polar explorers. In this he stood out during the period between the two World Wars, with Tom Longstaff and Raymond Priestley.'

Brian Roberts made his mark at SPRI for many years, combining a part-time job in the Institute with work at the Polar Desk of the Foreign Office in London.

Frank Debenham maintained an interest in Antarctica, acting as consultant to those venturing forth for the first time. Although he was recruited by Scott as assistant geologist and completed geological maps and collected specimens, he became fascinated, not unnaturally, in the polar environment, particularly by the glaciology of the area of Ross Island and Victoria Land. From 1932 onwards he gave lectures for Part Two of the geographical Tripos based on his experiences in 1910–12. His last academic paper was published just a month before he died in the *Journal of Glaciology* on 'The genesis of the McMurdo Ice Shelf, Antarctica'. It was appropriate that the offices of the headquarters of the International Glaciological Society (IGS) was at SPRI, and continues there today. For very many years the Secretary was a former student and geography graduate of Deb's, Hilda Richardson.

The general consensus of those close to Deb reinforces the view that he was an approachable man with a warm personality, a good organiser and an enthusiastic geographer. He believed in the educative value of the subject and strove to establish its place in the curriculum of courses of the University of Cambridge at a time when many of his 'ivory tower' friends considered that geography lacked the intellectual rigour of subjects such as mathematics and physics, or for that matter English literature or history. He had a special regard for the polar regions, both North and South, and supported undergraduate expeditions to the Arctic as well as to the Antarctic. Symptomatic of his passions was his determination to build, in Cambridge, two academies – a School of Geography and a Research Institute devoted to the polar regions. He succeeded with both and, even in his lifetime, they reached international reputations for fine teaching and excellent research. These institutions will remain to commemorate his zeal.

Although many of the tributes to Deb make reference to his eclectic interests and wise counsel, no one claimed for him a focussed academic specialism. He was not one of the early philosophers of his subject, nor did he seek to pioneer a new methodology. He was too early for the quantitative revolution in geography (principally the application of mathematical statistics) and eschewed references by continental sages to psychological analysis, perception and metaphor in the subject. He preferred a simplistic and practical approach in which place and distance were fixed by topographical measurements and cartographic representation. Of his over 100 published books and papers, it was his little book on *Map Making* (1936) that probably had the greatest circulation.

Undergraduates reading for the geography Tripos were obliged to take the preliminary examination to Part One at the end of their first year. The papers included questions on surveying, and part of their geographical techniques course was lectures in the use of the surveyor's chain, the prismatic compass and the plane-table, followed by exercises in and around Cambridge. The plane-table work was carried out by the beech woods of the low Gog Magog hills just to the south-east of Cambridge. Levelling with a theodolite was attempted in an area of small relative elevations on Coe Fen on the banks of the river Cam. Debenham had become proficient with these techniques whilst with Scott in the Antarctic, though Scott was originally somewhat sceptical of this instrument for field surveying. Debenham convinced Scott and members of the expedition of its value, not only at base camps but also on sledge journeys. Another geologist, Griffith Taylor, Australian by adoption, wrote in his own account of the *Terra Nova* Expedition:

'The plane-table is the instrument par excellence. Debenham deserves great credit for taking one south, for Capt. Scott was extremely sceptical as to their value on sledge journeys. In open country with a prominent peak (as a referring object) in the line of traverse-conditions such as one always gets in coastal work, the plane-table was extremely rapid and enabled Debenham to do excellent work each day. For details of the geology of a cape or cliff area the plane-table is simply magnificent.' (Taylor, 1977: Appendix)

Scott records in his diary (see Jones, 2005: 186) that Debenham was 'a well trained, sturdy worker, with a quiet meaning that carries conviction; he realises the conception of thoroughness and conscientiousness.'

Frank Debenham advised many of the expeditions of the Oxford and Cambridge Mountaineering and Explorers' Club in the inter-war years. They explored parts of Iceland, Greenland and Svalbard, and brought back original plane-table maps of their field study areas, and distance traverses made with a circular home-made meter pulled behind the sledge. Deb was adept at devising simple measuring instruments that were adequate for the field worker who was not a professional surveyor, particularly where illustrations were required for scientific papers. His methods were ideal for the field geologist, botanist, archaeologist and geographer. In 1936 he published in the journal *Geography* the article 'Cheaper plane-tables', for use in schools, and in the same year *Map Making*, a small handbook of surveying which became, for over 20 years, the standard text for amateur workers in the field and a companion work for those reading for degrees in geography.

As late as 1964 Deb published a paper in the *Geographical Journal* entitled 'A simple water level, for the measurement of relative heights and contouring'; it was contrived from a length of plastic hose pipe with upright laths of soft timber marked off in feet and inches, and cost a pittance compared to the professional surveyor's Sopwith staves and dumpy level with telescopic sights. Debenham found it perfectly adequate for surveying a large swamp in Central Africa, and private expeditions from Cambridge used it at various times in Nigeria, Sudan and Uganda where there was dense scrub or high grass. The device lends itself to schools and colleges short of cash but with plenty of practical zeal.

A manuscript fragment in the SPRI Archives, 'The plane-table in polar exploration', intended for publication in the *Geographical Journal* but never actually printed, was meant to encourage polar explorers to use this handy instrument. Debenham recognised that the plane-table was primarily an accessory, in these circumstances, to triangulation and general theodolite work, but where an area was being explored for the first time the plane-table could be quick and reliable. Surveying on polar sledge journeys is essentially traversing a strip of country outwards and homewards on roughly the same track. The plane-table can then be used to fix detail to add width to the survey whilst the limits of the traverse can be fixed astronomically. Some difficulties are presented by the weather and the other work to be accomplished; the surveying has to be done quickly and often in spare moments. All the plane-table sheets need not be surveyed at the same scale, base lines are easy to measure from sledge meter readings and the ends can be fixed later by theodolite.

On the 1910–13 British Antarctic Expedition (*Terra Nova*), Debenham's plane-table was entirely home-made: a drawing board about 15 × 20 in (38 × 51 cm), mounted on a stout camera tripod, clamped by a heavy screw fitting with large wings. The sighting instrument, the alidade, was a plain 15-in (38-cm) wooden ruler stiffened by a brass strip fastened to the bottom edge; the sights were fashioned out of two long brass hinges, and folded down for packing. The foresight was made of a fine wire soldered in place, but was later replaced by a simple waxed thread. An ivory scale rule completed the equipment. The trough compass was rarely used, as the survey area was close to the south magnetic pole. The whole was packed in a large double packet of stiff canvas, one for the table and the other for spare Bristol board sheets of drawing paper. Small accessories were kept in pockets outside. It all fitted neatly and tightly together to exclude snowdrift. The tripod was carried separately. This home-made plane-table was in constant use for two summers in the Antarctic and came to little harm.

On reflection, Deb suggested a tripod of aluminium for lightness with lugs fitted to the legs to prevent them sinking into the snow, and a lighter board with levels let into the corners for convenience. He accepted that at times professional accuracy had to be sacrificed for speed of travel, and that there was little point in fixing all halts on the traverse, which may be of no further use. The most valuable use was the fixing of distant points by triangulation and resection. In a private letter to Hugh Robert Mill (28 April 1921), Deb admits that the Antarctic surveying was 'badly planned and indifferently executed'. He maintains that McMurdo Sound needed to be completely resurveyed 'in the hands of good topographic surveyors, and not hydrographers'. He adds that 'Mt. Lister, daily in view of three Expeditions, was variously placed over an area of six miles [9.6 km]'. In the first account of the Expedition, published in 1913, the large map surveyed by Debenham, Griffith Taylor and Charles Wright on their western journey to Granite Harbour was inserted and shows the southern part fixed by theodolite angles and the northern section by plane-table angles (1913: 290).

★　★　★

The Debenham family was essentially English. The name Debenham seems to have originated in rural Suffolk and to have been there for many centuries. In his retirement, Deb made a detailed search for his ancestors and he published privately an elaborate line of descent in *Seven Centuries of Debenhams*. His research begins somewhat tentatively in the fourteenth century, but by the sixteenth, Debenhams were known in the village of Sapiston some time between 1520 and 1580. Since that date at least five generations of Debenhams have flourished in the area. It is appropriate etymologically, for the villages where the Debenham families were principally yeomen farmers lie at no great distance to the present small market town of Debenham, in the valley of the river Deben — though Sapiston and Ixworth Thorpe, where Deb's direct forebears were born, are closer to Bury St Edmunds.

The family was particularly prolific, marrying into other local families and each producing several children, often 12 or more. James Debenham (1764–1848) and his wife Mary, neé Nunn (1773–1862), produced a 'Debenham dozen', all born at Ixworth Thorpe over a period of 22 years, and all survived into adulthood. James and Mary were married in 1797 and produced one child each year from 1798 to 1808, and thence four more at intervals until 1820. By this time the greater mobility of the stage coach allowed for better prospects of marriage, and in any case the families were finding that there was not enough land for them all to become yeomen farmers. At this time a family grace was said:

> I thank the goodness and the grace
> That on my birth have smiled
> And made me, in this desert place
> A happy Debenham child.

One of the family tree's more tenuous links was the Bradfield branch. One son to achieve greatness became the enterprising businessman Sir Ernest Ridley Debenham (1865–1952), who created the well-known chain of retail department stores; he was created a baronet in 1931. His older brother, also a Frank Debenham, was the first director of the company from 1906 to 1912.

Deb managed to trace 518 relatives: 213 were born with the Debenham name, 116 male and 97 female; 18 were born in England, and 200 in Australia. The 'Debenham dozen' and their forefathers had a good expectation of life, the females averaging 60 years and the males 57. The average size of family overall was six, and in the present generation five. Deb adds in a note to his analysis that 'the men were usually good at sports, many took to business and the professions, and very few engaged in politics.'

The very detailed family tree which accompanies *Seven Centuries of Debenhams* measures 7 ft (2.3 m) in length, and 1 ft (0.3 m) in breadth. It is a tribute to Deb's tenacity and dedication: not only are the ages and relationships set against long time-lines, but each entry also includes details of education and chosen profession, so that the table becomes a kind of *Who's Who*. On completion of his thorough genealogical research, Deb threw a party in London and invited to it as many of the extant Debenhams as could easily come.

By the middle of the nineteenth century, the possibility of travelling further afield by train and even distant emigration overseas by steam ship could be considered. In the 1870s the country suffered the Great Agricultural Depression. Rural Suffolk was hit as badly as anywhere in England, land values fell, and many farmers became bankrupt. Four sons of the family of eight of John Martin Debenham (b. 1808), who was farming at Ixworth Thorpe, went to Australia. One of these was Deb's father, John Willmott Debenham (1852–98), who attended King Edward VI school at Bury St Edmund's, where he lodged with his aunt Margaret of the related Bullen family. By the time John Willmott was contemplating emigrating he was an ordained minister of the Church of England, but unhappily had contracted pneumonia. It was felt that a short stay in Australia would be good for his health, so he travelled there with his wife Edith, neé Cleveland, accompanied by his brother Arthur Alexander. They lived first in the Parish of Lithgow, New South Wales, and in the 1880s settled in Bowral, John Willmott as the local vicar living in the parsonage and, together with his wife, conducting the local school. It was here that Deb and his brothers and sisters were born, and they received their early education in their parents' schoolroom.

Bowral is a small township, established in 1861, south-west of Sydney, located in the Southern Highlands of New South Wales, but on the main railway line between Sydney and Canberra. It can be reached today by train from Sydney Country Station in 2 hours. (Bowral's principal claim to fame is as the birthplace of Sir Donald Bradman, the famous Australian cricketer; he is commemorated in the name of the present sports stadium.) Topographically the district is dominated by the 'Gib', so called because of its resemblance to the Rock of Gibraltar. It is clothed in gum trees and tree ferns to its summit, where Deb and his brother would race to the top. Today none of the descendants of the Bowral Debenhams live in the town, but several grandchildren, cousins and more distant relatives are still found in Australia.

Deb and his twin sister were born on 26 December 1883; sadly, Grace died in infancy. His elder brother Arthur became an engineer and assisted in the completion of Sydney Harbour Bridge. His younger brother Herbert was killed at Gallipoli in 1915. There were also three sisters, Essie, Joan and Peggy. When their father died in 1898, Deb's mother took over the running of their school.

Frank Debenham as a young man
in Sydney (Debenham family)

Deb continued his education at King's School, Parramatta, to the north of Sydney, leaving it in 1901 to enter Sydney University, where he graduated in 1904 with an ordinary degree BA in Classics. His first post was teaching Latin and Greek at Armidale School, a well-known New South Wales boarding school, still very popular today. He taught there for only a short time, returning to Sydney University in 1908, majoring in geology and petrology in 1910. The Professor of Geology at that time was Welsh-born Tannant William Edgeworth David, who had been with Sir Ernest Shackleton on the 1907–1909 British Antarctic (*Nimrod*) Expedition.

When Robert Falcon Scott was recruiting for his second expedition (*Terra Nova*), he approached Edgeworth David in Sydney for his recommendation of a young geologist. Scott appears to have wanted to associate the British Empire with his expedition: Canada was represented in the person of Charles Wright, a physicist, and Scott had already secured the services of Griffith Taylor as geologist, another Australian, working at that time in London and incidentally an old boy of Parramatta School. So it was on Edgeworth David's recommendation that Scott asked Frank Debenham to join him, thus by a strange but happy chance the young Debenham, who had not then travelled far outside his own south-east Australia, found himself bound for *Terra Australis Incognita*. Despite having very little experience of mountain climbing and none of snow and ice conditions, the door to an unexpected career was beginning to open.

At that time in London, Scott had virtually completed recruiting for the Antarctica voyage. He had received some 8,000 applications and had already appointed two geologists, Griffith Taylor and Raymond Priestley; there is no indication in Scott's account of the reasons for the appointment of a third. Scott interviewed Deb in a Sydney hotel, and with Edgeworth David's prior endorsement immediately offered him a place. Deb had been following the publicity about the expedition, but appears not to have made any formal application for a place. He was one of the youngest in the scientific party, and with the possible exception of Edward Nelson, biologist, and Apsley Cherry-Garrard, assistant zoologist, the least experienced. Cherry-Garrard had been recruited in similarly exceptional circumstances (that is, by personal recommendation), but he was a rich young man and able to contribute substantially to the costs of the expedition. Deb's chance came happily, but unexpectedly. Although he was recruited to contribute to the geological investigations, he undertook also to carry out basic surveying and mapping, hence he made the business of plane-tabling and theodolite measurements one of his principal preoccupations.

For Deb it was to be a completely new experience, the forming of new friendships, the regime of expedition life and its discipline, and the appreciation of ice landscapes. This would prove to be the most formative of his early life experience, and an icon for his later development as geographer, scientist and educator. He was, however, to witness the ultimate grief and poignancy at the failure of the Pole party to return from the major objective of the expedition – the conquest of the South Pole.

After telegraphing the dreadful news to the world and giving a succession of interviews to the press, the scientists and crew were signed off. Deb contacted his family and then left New Zealand in 1913 with Charles Wright. They travelled to England by way of Vancouver, and returned to stay first with the family of Raymond Priestley at Tewkesbury, where Griffith Taylor joined them. Whilst there, they began the task of compiling the expedition and scientific reports. These were first drafted in a room which was part of the school where Raymond Priestley's father was headmaster. The four Antarctic explorers – Deb, Griff, Wright and Priestley – agreed that Cambridge would be the best place in which to complete the reports. At first this might seem a quixotic move, for the association that they had with Professor Edgeworth David in Sydney would have provided scope for organising the geology specimens in Australia, but friendships had been forged in Antarctica and they were all returning to Cambridge to pursue academic careers. Thus to Cambridge they relocated, a decision which would prove seminal in all their lives. But before this happened, Charles Wright had fallen in love with Ray Priestley's sister, Edith, and they became engaged to be married. A little later, Griffith Taylor followed suit by marrying Ray's other sister, Doris, so binding permanently a 'group of four' – one British, one Canadian and two Australians – who had first met in the icy wastes of Antarctica (Wright, 1974: 215).

However, these were momentous times in the history of Europe, for the expedition party was arriving back in England as the signs of impending armed conflict became apparent. Those who had been seconded from the Royal Navy rejoined their units, and others returned to academic or civilian life. Before long, however, war would be declared and virtually all of the expedition party, to a man, volunteered to enlist; some who had survived Antarctica were tragically killed in action.

Deb entered Gonville and Caius College in Cambridge, following in the footsteps of his hero Edward Adrian Wilson (Uncle Bill), and began to sort his Antarctic papers and call on other members of the expedition for further material. Subsequently, he joined the King Edward's Horse regiment as a trooper. In June 1914 he returned to Australia to attend a meeting of the Australian branch of the British Association for the Advancement of Science, but arrived only to hear that war had been declared in Europe. He returned home on the same ship that had brought him, took a commission and was appointed Lieutenant in the 7th Oxfordshire and Buckinghamshire Light Infantry. He joined his regiment on 17 October 1914, and was first billeted in Keble College, Oxford. By December he had been promoted to the rank of Captain. He then spent several months in training, and in July 1915 was promoted to the rank of Major. In September he left for France, in charge of D Company, and after seven weeks the battalion was transferred via Marseilles to Salonika in Greece. At first everything was quiet and on 10 May 1916 he wrote to his former Antarctic comrade, Cherry-Garrard, who was recovering from colitis: 'Not much happening here; very different from France.' Cherry suffered for most of his life from recurrent attacks of colitis, and this, added to his genetic shortsightedness, produced frequent periods of melancholic neurosis towards the end of his life. Deb kept a regular (if not too frequent) correspondence with Cherry, and always addressed him by the familiar 'My Dear Old Cherry', his letters usually containing a bit of ragging about Cherry's bachelor state and enquiries of 'any girl friends yet'?

By August of 1916 Deb's battalion was coming under sporadic fire, and in one of the patrols on the Salonika front Deb was blown up on Horseshoe Hill, Lake Doiran, by a 5.9-in shell, which burst beside him. He was seriously injured, suffered shell-shock and invalided home. After a long spell in hospital he returned to his unit at Fort Purbrook, Cosham, Hampshire, though he was subject to recurring bouts of severe headaches and increasing deafness which was to plague him for the rest of his life. At Fort Purbrook he was supposed to take things easy, but he wrote to Cherry on 5 May 1917:

'I am here on "Light Duties" which is a fiction. From 8.20 p.m. to 2.30 a.m., am racing round the Portsmouth forts inspecting guards; also

inspected every ward in two hospitals in the afternoon, one of which for
V.D. Also I run a Company – Young Soldiers Training Batt. – and am
President of Courts Martial in my spare time!'

He asked Cherry in the same letter for the address of Dennis Lillie, the biologist
from *Terra Nova*, in order to visit him as he was living nearby, and in a light-hearted
conclusion exclaims 'What ho, the Broke! Have you heard any details?' This was a
reference to their former colleague, Lieut. Edward R.G.R. Evans (Teddy Evans),
Captain of *Terra Nova* and second-in-command to Capt. Scott. He had distinguished
himself in the Battle of Jutland for his brilliant control of the warship *Broke*, had been
promoted to Admiral, and gained considerable public acclaim.

When Deb was in Melbourne following the return from Antarctica, he stayed
briefly with the Lempriere family and became good friends with them. They seem to
have followed Deb to England, for in May 1916 he refers to writing to them in
Paignton, South Devon, where one daughter, Midge, was nursing and two others
were in pharmacy. A fourth daughter also living in England, whom Deb now met for
the first time, was Dorothy Lucy Lempriere. They fell in love and were married on
27 January 1917 at St Philip's Church, Kensington, whilst Deb was still recuperating
from his war injuries.

In November 1917, Dorothy gave birth to their first child, a daughter named
Barbara Lempriere. They lived in a village close to Fort Purbrook, but Deb gradually
became increasingly frustrated: on the one hand he was conscious of his obligations
to complete the scientific and cartographic reports of Scott's expedition, and on the
other he felt acutely a responsibility to his regiment through his enforced absence
from active duties. He communicated these embarrassments to Cherry in a letter
dated 25 March 1918, from No. 6 Camp Rollestone, Wiltshire. He had been with a
training battalion for six to eight months, but was obliged to appear regularly at a
medical board, where each time he had been adjudged well enough only for 'home
service'. He adds that an officer could not have permanent home service: he must be
considered fit for 'general service duties' or discharged.

Deb had decided to lie about the state of his health to avoid this judgement: 'I
must be prepared if the catastrophe comes.' It is not clear whether this refers to a
down-turn in the course of the war or the prospect of discharge from the army. In
any case, he hoped his colonel would allow him to proceed with the editing of the
scientific reports.

Deb asked about the address of a Col. H.G. Lyons who had been appointed, in
1914, secretary of the Antarctic expedition's publications committee. Both Evans and
Atch (Edward L. Atkinson) had suggested that Cherry should write the official
account of the expedition, and Cherry had welcomed this. The war had delayed the
collection of written reports, as most of the expedition members were in the armed
services, and there was a danger of manuscripts becoming lost. Cherry had sent some

of the scientific materials to Lyons by mistake, and this was now Deb's urgent concern. Both Deb and Cherry were becoming impatient with Lyons. Cherry-Garrard eventually produced the magnificent *The Worst Journey in the World*, with the help of his friend and close neighbour George Bernard Shaw acting as literary advisor, and Deb continued writing his reports in Cambridge. Deb maintained to Cherry that he needed a job worth £300 a year or 'we'll starve'. He 'didn't want to beg the War Office to save us from the "work 'us"!' Deb, Dorothy and little Barbara were now living at Highfield House, Shrewton, Wiltshire, a 'nice, seclusive house down in Wilts. – but expensive'.

By May of that year things were quieter, with fewer recruits to train. Deb and his family lived a rustic existence, planting peas and potatoes and running a farm of half an acre. He asked Cherry how he was getting on with history, 'still discussing social reform or devolution with Shaw? You really must drop that man, he is several centuries too early for us ordinary people.' He told him that Tryggve Gran (the Norwegian member of the expedition) 'has married an actress at last, how ever did she catch him? . . . Re marriage, we are all looking towards you, you know; you've had enough examples set you now, good and bad, from Expedition fellows.' In fact, Cherry, although not without several girlfriends at this time, married late in life: in 1939 he married Angela Turner, who was almost 23 years of age at the time and Cherry 53. Cherry died in 1959, and Angela (later Mathias) only in 2005.

In December 1918 Deb could see that the end of his military career was in sight. He considered resuming his academic career as he believed he would be demobilised at the end of January 1919. There seemed to be no place to return to other than Cambridge. There he could finish the reports of the expedition, sort and arrange his geological specimens, and moreover have the friendship of former colleagues Raymond Priestley, Charles (Silas) Wright and Griffith Taylor, who were also returning to take up academic positions in Cambridge University. He wrote to Cherry: 'I will look for the most stylish hovel we can afford in Cambridge, and whack away at the Report till it is finished.'

He then had an unsympathetic run-in with Col. Lyons, whom he described as 'a blighter'. Lyons had told Deb that the material for the reports was all dependent upon Deb and his friends, and that he (Deb) could expect no material help from him. Deb disclosed that he was 'sniffing around for a part time job in Cambridge, and with help from the dons at Caius may get one. Silas is in the same racket.' He believed that 'working at the rocks' would give him plenty of kudos and a job 'somewhere in the world of rocks'. He confessed that 'the mere sight of a pile of road metal makes me cheerful now.' He hoped to finish two of the draft chapters of Cherry's book and motor over 'to have a good yarn with him'.

Deb returned to Cambridge early in 1919 and renewed his college association with Gonville and Caius. Fortunately he was able to find something more than 'a hovel' in and around Cambridge for his family. In 1919 he was writing from 48

Lensfield Road, a location to figure very largely in the remainder of his life; then in 1921 from 152 Chesterton Road, Cambridge; from here the family moved, in the 1930s, to The Limes, Milton Road and then successively to The Lodge, Waterbeach, Cambridge, then 23 Cranmer Road, 5 Millington Road, and finally to Herne Lodge, 6 St Eligius Street, from where the walk to the new Institute was only five minutes and to the School of Geography no more than ten.

By now Deb's family had grown to six children, four girls and two boys. Barbara (1917) was the eldest. She attended the Perse School for Girls in Cambridge, and was recruited to the Foreign Office (actually MI6) during the Second World War and was seconded to the New York office, officially as a secretary. She returned to England later in the war and joined the ATS before being seconded by the Foreign Office to work in Singapore.

Kenneth Barry Debenham (always known as Barry) was born in 1920, educated privately at Canford School, and trained as a chartered accountant but joined the Royal Air Force at the start of the war and became a fighter pilot in the Battle of Britain, where he was shot down and seriously burned. He was treated at the special

The Debenham Family, 1939 at Cranmer Road: *back*, Barry, Barbara, Brian; *middle*, Audrey, Dorothy, Deb; *front*, Ann, June (Debenham family)

burns unit in East Grinstead, Surrey, where he was visited by Dr Hugh Robert Mill and his wife Freda, who lived close by at Hill Crest, Dorman's Park. (Dr Mill had already established a reputation as a very able geographer and historian of polar exploration. He held the position of Librarian of the Royal Geographical Society for very many years, was a frequent visitor to Cambridge, and became a highly influential and good friend to Deb, especially in the establishment of both the School of Geography and the Research Institute.) Barry was grounded for a time after his convalescence, though anxious to fly again as soon as possible. He was sick with disappointment at being given the post of flying instructor, and had told his father 'It is far more dangerous training Englishmen than fighting Germans in the air'. At last in 1943 he was allowed to join a squadron in the Mediterranean, based in Malta, confessing to Deb that it took him some time to regain his confidence to fly fighter planes, but despite this he rose to command his Squadron.

In January 1944 Deb wrote to Dr Mill that he and the family were anxious about Barry, who had been posted missing from Italy on 16 December 1943. On 22 January, Deb and Dorothy learned that there was no further news other than Barry may have come down over Albania, but it was not until the autumn that the Air Ministry advised that both he and his Wing Commander were lost, presumed dead. They had been flying a special mission over Albania. On 8 October 1944 Deb commented in a letter to Dr Mill: 'To me there is something almost unreal about these gallant reckless fighter pilots and I still wonder how a son of mine could have summoned a courage and achieved a skill which I don't think I could ever have achieved. But that pride is the solace one seeks.' Barry and his Wing Commander were never heard of again. All the Debenham family were devastated by the loss of a son and brother.

The Scott Polar Research Institute closed to the public from September 1939. This allowed, in 1942, research to take place in the compilation of Naval Intelligence Handbooks to assist in military operations. At that time Deb was looking forward to the return of the Institute and remarked to Mill that 'the end of the war is in sight and I hope to open in June. There is youth, restless from the war, who will be wanting further adventure and in the Navy and RAF a great deal of Arctic experience.' If Barry could not come home, Deb had the consolation of creating a peacetime environment for other young men to carry the torch of exploration to polar places.

Of the other children, Audrey Margaret (1922) was educated at a small private school, Birklands, started nursing but then joined the WRNS in July 1942, served in East Africa, and by October 1944 was an officer serving in Colombo. Herbert Brian (Brian) was born in 1923, attended the Leys School in Cambridge, entered the army and served in India before moving to Australia where he became a teacher, and studied and taught later in the University of Brisbane. June (1925), like Barbara, attended the Perse School and considered taking a degree in geography but entered the nursing profession instead, and Frances Ann (1928) had her early education at

Godolphin School, and then studied dramatic art; she eventually emigrated to South Africa.

Of the houses inhabited by all the English Debenham families, the most gracious home was Cheshunt Park in Hertfordshire. It was a typical Victorian house built for a prosperous middle-class family, and the scene of many family gatherings. For 50 years an annual cricket match was played against the local village team. The last one took place in 1940, the side being captained by Frank Debenham from Australia, and their side won by the 'deadly bowling' of 18-year-old Brian, over for the day from Haileybury (*Seven Centuries of Debenhams*).

Frank Debenham proved to be very popular, not only amongst his academic colleagues within Cambridge, but also in the wider circles of British geography through the Royal Geographical Society. As one of the surviving members of Scott's last expedition he had achieved a certain celebrity status, and was regarded one of the few authorities of Antarctic exploration. He was not only Professor of Geography and Director of the Scott Polar Research Institute, but also a tireless member of numerous University committees, and as a College Fellow, a long-serving member of Caius. Frank and Dorothy Debenham were genial hosts and counsellors in Cambridge to countless students and colleagues over many years. Deb died in 1965, and Dorothy was killed in a motoring accident in 1973.

CHAPTER 2

With Scott in the Antarctic

In the first decade of the twentieth century there was much international interest in the Antarctic continent – *Terra Australis Incognita* – particularly since the sixth meeting in London of the International Geographical Congress in 1895 had declared that all nations in the world should endeavour to explore the scientific value of Antarctica: its continent, oceans and surrounding islands. Great Britain had an early interest; Capt. James Cook in his second circumnavigation in *Resolution* crossed the Antarctic Circle for the first time on 17 January 1773, reached latitude 71° S, and landed on South Georgia. It was not until the sealing voyages of the 1820s that the islands of the South Shetlands and the Antarctic Peninsula were first exploited by British vessels.

After the encouragement of this 1895 meeting of the International Geographical Congress, six national expeditions were mounted, both to extend Antarctic science and, through new discoveries, to improve Antarctic cartography. The first to set off was the Belgian expedition, 1897–99, led by Lt Adrien de Gerlache de Gomery in the *Belgica*, which explored the Antarctic Peninsula. Between 1901 and 1904 Capt. Robert Falcon Scott led the *Discovery* Expedition to Antarctica and attained a latitude of 82° 16' S before being forced to return. From 1902 to 1904, the Scottish National Antarctic Expedition (*Scotia*), led by William Speirs Bruce, explored the South Orkney Islands and conducted a detailed oceanographic survey of the Weddell Sea, discovering Coats Land on the continent. Under the command of Drygalski, Germany sent the *Gauss* to the east of the continent in 1901–1903, and during the same period the Swedes sent Otto Nordenskjöld in their ship *Antarctica* to the Antarctic Peninsula. France was active in the same area under Dr Jean-Baptiste Charcot, sailing in the *Français* in 1903–1905 and again in the *Pourquoi Pas?* in 1908–1910. There was a further major British Antarctic Expedition in 1907–1909, led by Ernest Henry Shackleton, which attempted to reach the South Pole; they attained 'furthest south' within 1° 37' of the pole on 9 January 1909.

The British Antarctic Expedition (1910–1913) led by Robert Falcon Scott had honourable antecedents, and Scott knew that the British public and the news media were expecting him to lead an assault on the Pole. On his way south Scott called a press meeting in Sydney, Australia, to ask for further funds and said:

'Gentlemen, if you ask me what is the use of reaching the Pole, I can only answer that the advantage to be gained is practically nil. But there is a sentimental reason which should outweigh all questions of use. The English nation has always been the leader in exploration and it seems contrary to all traditions of the nation to stand by while other nations do the work.'

He freely admitted that the first object before the expedition was to reach the Pole, but he always intended that the expedition should be best remembered by its scientific work, and by far the greater portion of the funds subscribed was allotted to the scientific side (SPRI MS280/18).

At this time he feared no rivalry from Roald Amundsen and the Norwegians, for Amundsen had all along maintained that he was headed for the Arctic and the North Pole.

Farewell tea party in the Geology Museum, University of Sydney, 22 October 1910 (Debenham family): from left, *standing* Edgeworth David, Griffith Taylor, Raymond Priestley, W. N. Benson, unknown, Leo Cotton; *sitting*, Fanny Cohen (demonstrator), two unknown; *front row*, Frank Debenham, W. S. Dun, Catherine Smith (demonstrator)

Terra Nova sailed from her moorings at West India Dock on the Thames at 5.00 p.m. on 1 June 1910. She was seen off by Sir Robert Clements and Lady Markham, amongst many others, and passed Scott's old ship, *Discovery*, as she moved downstream. Scott and his wife, Kathleen, left the ship at Greenhithe in order to clear up the administrative arrangements for the expedition and to try to raise more money for it. Scott would rejoin the ship temporarily at Portland in the English Channel to steam to Cardiff, in South Wales, in order to fill her bunkers with a free supply of best Welsh coal. They were given a splendid farewell banquet in the Royal Hotel, Cardiff, and left for the Antarctic on 15 June. Scott left London together with Kathleen in *R.M.S. Saxon* on 17 June, overtaking *Terra Nova*, which he was to rejoin in Cape Town.

Scott had purchased *Terra Nova* from the Bowring Bros. of St John's, Newfoundland. She had been built in Dundee in 1884, and was considered the best of the Scottish whalers. Scott had first seen her when she had come to the rescue of *Discovery*, stuck fast in the Antarctic ice, in 1904, but the ship was now much battered and required a complete overhaul. She was sold to him for £12,500, but he realised that there was much to do in the refitting process. Some of the new planking seemed to have been inferior, as by the time the ship reached New Zealand serious leaks were apparent. The vessel, a three-masted wooden ship of 347 tons gross, had to be dry-docked in Lyttelton and the stores restowed under the supervision of Petty Officer Edgar Evans. When Lieut. 'Teddy' Evans, who was to command the ship, first saw her in West India Dock, he exclaimed 'She looked so small and out of place'. Yet this little vessel had to carry to the Antarctic enough stores for an expedition lasting for two, possibly three, years. Deb first saw the ship in Lyttelton harbour and commented 'She looked remarkably small considering the load she would have to carry'. The ship would take on more stores in New Zealand, together with the dogs and the ponies, to be unloaded on the ice-shelf, and then would return to New Zealand and go back to Antarctica with provisions for the second year; nevertheless she was required to take, from London, the basic supplies of tinned and dried foodstuffs, tents and sledges for the exploratory journeys, paraffin, oil and coal for light and heat and power, the prefabricated structures for constructing the base hut, all scientific apparatus, engineering and building spares, and a small library of books and records for recreation. In addition, Scott was taking three motorised sledges and the generous gift of a player-piano. Not surprisingly, observers in Cardiff, at the ship's leaving, considered her 'low in the water', and when *Terra Nova* left Port Chalmers, the outport for Lyttleton, with an even greater cargo, port officials must have looked the other way when inspecting the plimsoll line.

Like most of the members recruited by Scott, Deb kept a set of journals throughout the expedition. The following account is based on these personal journals, kept now at SPRI. They comprise:

Vol. 1 – 26 November 1910 to 18 January 1911
Vol. 2 – 19 January to 8 March 1911
Vol. 3 – 14 April to 1 November 1911 and 1 March to 25 November 1912
Vol. 4 – 23–26 December 1912 (Mt. Erebus to Cape Royds)

A transcription of these, edited by Deb's daughter June Debenham Back, can be found, with some additional material from family sources, in *Quietland*. A supplementary source is *Incomplete Narrative of the British Antarctic (Terra Nova) Expedition 1910–1913*, which can be found in the SPRI Archives.

Frank Debenham and Griffith Taylor made their own way to join the ship in Lyttleton, New Zealand, although they could have joined *Terra Nova* when she called at Melbourne en route from Cape Town. As assistant geologist, Deb had very little in the way of special apparatus, just a geological hammer and his survey equipment, which fitted conveniently into one canvas pack. He had also brought along with him his wooden flute. After the preliminary introductions to Lieut. Victor Campbell, the mate, Edgar Evans and other members of the expedition, Deb, Griff and Charles Wright (known hereafter as Silas) paid heed to Scott's sensible suggestion that they should start to learn their mountain craft and the experience of crossing ice and snow terrain amongst the Southern Alps of New Zealand. They travelled to a government accommodation hut, The Hermitage, under Mount Sefton on 8 November 1910 and climbed on to the Mueller Glacier, some 1,200 ft (365 m) up the massif, and glissaded down about 1,000 ft (304 m). Two days later they began an extended climb, 14 miles (18.5 km) to Ball Hut at 3,400 ft (1,036 m) above sea level, and 500 ft (152 m) above the Tasman Glacier led by their native guide, Graham (it is not clear whether this is a first name or a patronymic).

On 11 November the same party set out for the source of the Tasman Glacier, the Hochstetter Dome. Towards the top they had their first instruction in ropework: tied on to a climbing rope, with Graham in the lead, cutting ice steps. At the top Silas freed himself to take photos. Deb wrote in his diary, 'He is the most delightfully happy-go-

Deb's geological hammer (Debenham family)

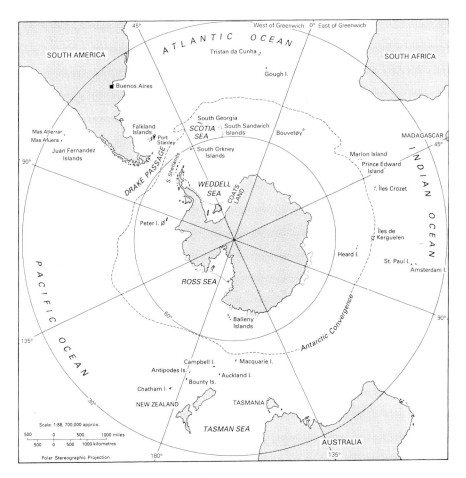

Map of Antarctica and surrounding areas (P. Speak)

lucky person I've ever met. He isn't used to photography and it's great fun seeing him take a photo. But nothing can put him out of humour.' They glissaded again over the last few hundred feet and went back to Ball Hut on ski. It was a fairly propitious beginning for them into the landscapes of icy mountains and glaciers. Deb had a good impression of Griff and Silas in these conditions; both were to become life-long friends, and spend important time with Deb in Cambridge.

Deb had also learned a salutary lesson about snow and ice glare. He had forgotten to take any snow goggles with him and by the evening he could hardly see; his eyes hurt terribly. The next day a horse was found for Deb; he rode back, virtually blindfold, all the way to the Hermitage. They were then recalled by Scott, and on 21 November made their way back to Christchurch and eventually to *Terra Nova*.

All was ready for departure on 5 December. *Terra Nova* was, at last, under steam and sail, bound for Antarctica and, all being well for the chosen few, the South Pole. On the ship the complement consisted of 19 officers and scientists and 14 men forming the shore party, and a further 32 officers and men in the ship's party who would return to New Zealand once the initial settlement in Antarctica had been established. This total figure should be compared to Amundsen's complement on the Norwegian ship *Fram*: 19 men all told, compared to the 65 on *Terra Nova*. *Fram* was 440 tons (447 tonnes), 126 ft (38.4 m) overall, 35 ft (10.6 m) beam; *Terra Nova* 747 tons (759 tonnes), 187 ft (56.9 m). overall, and 31 ft (9.4 m) beam. *Fram* was diesel driven, whilst *Terra Nova* was a steam-powered vessel, very demanding on manpower. At that time *Fram* had already reached McMurdo Sound and was moored at Framheim in the Bay of Whales, adventitiously for a party intent on a 'race for the Pole'. For a route to the South Pole, the distance was considerably shorter from Framheim than from Ross Island where Scott was heading. All those on board *Terra Nova* knew then that Amundsen had reversed his decision to seek the North Pole and was bound for the southernmost end of the earth instead.

The accounts of the rivalry between Scott and Amundsen in their search for the Pole have been told in innumerable critical volumes and articles of exploration. There is no good reason to attempt to add to these; the stories are so well known and the advantages and disadvantages often repeated. The eulogies and criticisms of both Roald Amundsen and Capt. Scott may well go on forever. In this book we shall concentrate on the part played by Frank Debenham, and the influence that Scott's expedition of 1910–13 had on his subsequent career.

After only two full days at sea, the first of the many serious adversities occurred that were to strike this expedition. If the worst had taken place, virtually all might have been lost before *Terra Nova* had reached the Antarctic pack ice. On 1 December the ship encountered a fierce storm, one of the many deep depressions known to occur along the polar front in that section of the Southern Ocean. *Terra Nova* was a small ship, and the distance between the crests of the waves so great that the ship was continually awash from stem to stern. Moreover, the ship had a roll of up to 50 degrees, and of course at this time had no stabilisers, thus by combining plunging and rolling motions the decks were continually drenched in sea water, and below decks 'at every roll the water, a foot or so deep, would sweep like a young Niagara across the room'. Deb, Priestley and Cherry were dreadfully seasick, and at first kept to their bunks until on 2 December Simpson called them out, seasick or not, to give a hand. They found the engine room awash and all hands pumping like mad, as the over-weighted ship had sprung a leak. Gradually the main pump and even the hand pumps seized, clogged by coal dust, and the fires were drawn as the sea water rose to the level of the stoke-hold plates. All had to take spells of two hours each, passing buckets of water up from the

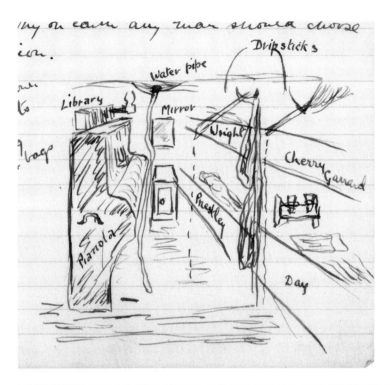

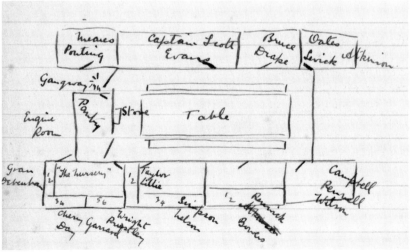

Original sketches by Deb in the hut at Cape Evans (SPRI)

fiercely hot engine room to the bitingly cold main deck. Deb and Priestley worked together and after five two-hour spells the water was low enough to get at the bottom of the pumps. Evans and Simpson cut a hole through an iron bulkhead to reach them and managed to clean and restore the steam pumps to active service.

The ship had been hoved-to for about 40 hours, and by 4.00 p.m. on 3 December was steaming once more. A quantity of coal and petrol had been lost at sea, and two ponies and one dog washed overboard. By 5 December calm weather had arrived, but it had been a close call between survival and disaster. The ship not only leaked through the bottom timbers, but also through the deck planking so that most of the bunks were uncomfortably wet (except, fortuitously, Deb's and Gran's). The engineer, Bernard Day, had rigged an ingenious set of piped channels to divert the drips from above to avoid drenching some of the bunks.

There was now a good spell of fine weather, broken only by occasional showers of snow and moderate winds. At this point Deb relates in his diary his special musical skill:

'About 5 o'clock this afternoon it fell dead calm and it was quite warm in the sun, although unpleasantly cold in the shade, while playing the flute to the penguins soon gave me chilled digits. After the penguins had had enough of the music I played jigs and polkas to the fellows and they made themselves warm quickly while I froze.'

Deb's wooden flute
(Debenham family)

Captain Scott's birthday dinner, 6 June 1911 (SPRI)

The lull gave them all an opportunity to relax – the officers, scientists and crew – and to re-establish the daily round of deck chores, particularly the care of the ponies and dogs. An air of expectancy was general, as daylight lengthened the further south they steamed, and the first icebergs appeared together with their first sightings of penguins, other sea birds, whales and seals.

They crossed the Antarctic Circle on 10 December. On Christmas Day the morning chores had to be completed, such as an hour's pumping from 6.30–7.30 a.m., before they decked the ward room with brilliantly coloured sledge flags. The ship's company assembled for the traditional service and lustily sang all the hymns. An excellent Christmas dinner was enjoyed:

> Mulligatawny Soup
> Fricassee of Penguin
> Roast Beef and York Ham
> Plum Pudding and Tartlets
> Almonds Ginger Chocolates
> Champagne and Liqueurs

There was only one toast, 'Absent Friends'. As Deb records, this was sung with 'great empresse'. Afterwards, community singing was enlivened by solos, and Gran made a speech on behalf of Norway. 'I do think in my mind of Capt. Scott this time next year sitting quite close to the South Pole, a little frost bitten on the nose perhaps but very warm inside. We do always say in our country that bad luck in the first of an expedition do mean good luck in the end.' It seemed a most appropriate and politic speech, as Gran was the only Norwegian on Scott's expedition and all those on board were aware that Roald Amundsen was probably already landed on the ice in McMurdo Sound and preparing for his attempt at the Pole.

New Year's Day passed without much ceremony, but the first glimpses were obtained of Victoria Land and the Admiralty Range of the Antarctic mainland. In the close confines of the ship, familiarity was quickly achieved and Deb placed on record in his diary the personnel in the ward room:

Capt. Scott, the 'Owner'
Lieut. Evans (Teddy), Second-in-Command
Dr Wilson (Bill or Uncle Bill), Doctor, biologist and artist
Dr Atkinson (Atch), Surgeon and helper with ponies
Lieut. Campbell (Mr Mate), Leader of the Eastern Party
Lieut. Bowers (Birdie), in charge of all stores
Capt. Oates (Soldier), in charge of ponies
Meares (Mother), in charge of dogs
Ponting (Ponko), Photographer in chief
Simpson (Sunny Jim), Meteorologist
Wright (Silas), Chemist and ice physicist, from Canada
Nelson (Marie), Biologist and extra motor sledge driver
Day (Bernard), Engineer in charge of motors
Priestley (R.E.P.), Geologist
Taylor (Griff), Geologist
Levick (Tofferino or Old Sport), Doctor of the Eastern Party
Cherry-Garrard (Cherry), Assistant to Dr Wilson
Lieut. Pennell (Penelope), Navigating officer
Lillie, Biologist – not in shore party
Bruce, Mrs Scott's brother – not in shore party
Drake, Paymaster and Secretary – not in shore party
Gran, Norwegian, expert on skis

Note that Scott maintained the regulation division between naval officers (and scientists) who ate together in the ward room, and the crew who messed separately. This division was kept in the base hut on the Antarctic continent.

The *Terra Nova* explorers outside Scott's base camp, Cape Evans, October 1911 (SPRI)

Deb added that he had not had the chance yet to form the same close relationship with the crewmen of *Terra Nova*; this would come as soon as they began unloading the ship's cargo at their eventual destination. It should also be noted that the creation of an Eastern Party was not possible in the end and so became the Northern Party instead.

At last, on 3 January 1911, the whole of Ross Island came into view with its three volcanic peaks: Mounts Erebus and Terror, first discovered by the Scottish explorer James Clark Ross in the British naval expedition of 1839–43, and a lower peak named Terra Nova after Scott's ship. After reconnoitring the barrier ice for some time, Scott made fast at 8.00 a.m. on 4 January, opposite a low headland. He had hoped to land at Cape Crozier, but this new location was more convenient, and has since become known as Cape Evans. Now all the ship's company were mustered to begin the difficult task of unloading the cargo. The three motor sledges were first, then the ponies and the dogs: the motor sledges were all swung overboard by rigging blocks and tackle; the ponies were hoisted from the ship, with difficulty, in horse boxes (see Jones, 2005: 71); and the dogs by bowline. An attendant line of curious penguins watched the whole proceedings.

The ship was moored one and a half miles from the landing place, so all the stores had to be sledged across the pack ice. At this point Deb had his introduction to dog driving, pulling five sledges with pony fodder and emergency rations in his first trip, and this routine carried on for three days, working 14 hours a day until all the heavy stores were landed. By 12 January the exterior of the base hut was finished, constructed of triple walls and heavily insulated; it promised to be very cosy and warm. Built on the northern side was the stable block, with easy access from the interior of the hut. The scientists and officers were given 6 × 4 ft (1.8 × 1.2 m) for their own living and sleeping space, and the others were separated from them by a wall of packing cases. Deb wrote to his mother in Bowral of his first impressions of his colleagues:

'It would be hard to give you a general impression of what I think of it all. I am only just beginning to feel a part of the expedition, as thanks to my reserve and to my seasickness and the strangeness of things it took me a long time to get on anything like familiar terms with them all and even now I am afraid I am excessively quiet and I expect they don't know what to make of me. My hard work these last few days however has given a good impression, I think, and several who looked askance at me before, are now hail fellow well met. Dr. Wilson is very good to me and thanks to some success with the ponies Capt. Oates is a good friend. It is too early to say much of what I think of them all yet and I have already had to alter my opinions of several of them. But in the main they are a splendid lot of fellows . . . If I were asked to pick out the best all round men, I should place Wilson easily first, then Campbell, Pennell, Oates and Bowers. Priestley has been just a little disappointing, and his prominence as a man with previous experience seems to have disturbed his equilibrium a little. . . . Griff is not getting on too well, in fact I think he is the only man who is not one of the party so to speak. He is rather selfish in small matters and his few ungentlemanly habits rather jar on the collection of real gentlemen we have here. I get on with him alright and I'm afraid that will mean I shall have to share a cubicle with him, and he is not a pleasant cabin mate. Day is a rattling good chap, Nelson (biologist) not so good. Atkinson is very kind-hearted but doesn't seem very strong. Capt. Scott is a very thorough leader, tho' he has not commanded the ship; he is very humane too, and has counteracted several orders of Campbell's who believes in getting the last ounce out of every man at all times.'

These were early days but Deb, one of the youngest and least experienced members of the expedition, was beginning to feel the pulse of a party which might need to stay together for over two years. But with cheerful optimism he concludes

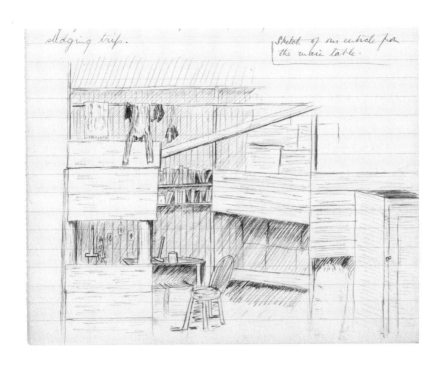

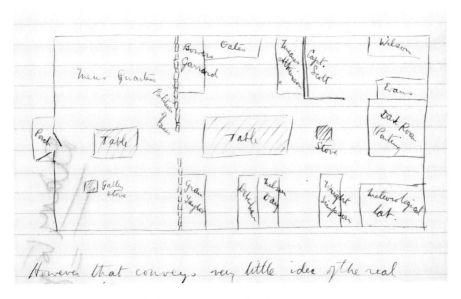

Original sketches by Deb in the hut at Cape Evans (SPRI)

his letter: 'I think there is little chance of our staying down another year, and if only things go fairly well on the Pole Journey I think they must reach it.' Clearly Deb saw himself as fulfilling a supporting role and did not consider himself likely to be selected for the final accolade.

After one week's hard work sledging from ship to shore, the cargo was well stored at Cape Evans and Capt. Scott could begin to redistribute further supplies to depot camps. All hands free to do so sledged fodder, on 5 January, from the ship to Camp One of the Southern Depot Party. Deb and his scientific colleagues made this an opportunity to get fit for their own sledging expedition, and they all crossed over the five miles to explore Shackleton's old Discovery hut by climbing through a broken window.

Scott had conducted discussions with all the scientists on *Terra Nova* during the long journey from New Zealand about the desirable areas of research, and made preliminary allocations of personnel. His general strategy was to divide the work into a number of journeys:

> Autumn journeys, January–April 1911
> The Barrier Depot Party to establish One Ton Depot
> The Western Party to examine the Royal Society Range
> The Eastern Party to examine King Edward VII Land (later re-named the Northern Party).

> Winter Party, July 1911
> Cape Crozier to search for Emperor penguin's egg

> Spring expeditions – November 1911 to March 1912
> The second Western Party to Granite Harbour
> The Southern Party – assault on the Pole

The Barrier Depot Party left on 26 January 1911, and the next day the ship left Glacier Tongue with both the Western and Eastern Parties. The latter were left at Butter Point, but the Eastern Party, under the leadership of Victor Campbell, was unable to land at King Edward Land, and instead disembarked at Cape Adare to commence a second geological expedition that was destined to last many months in the fiercest conditions; those left behind at Cape Evans considered them to be totally lost.

The Western Party was led by Griff, supported by Deb, Silas and Teddy Evans, who acted as sledgemaster and cook. Scott had originally placed the leadership in the hands of Ponting, but after a contretemps with Griff, Scott reversed his decision (Pound, 1968: 221). Taylor was principal geologist, assisted by Deb whose main job was the collection of specimens, and Silas was principally a glaciologist. They had planned provisions to be away for eight weeks, returning to Hut Point and then back to Cape Evans. Deb wrote to his mother on 20 January 1911:

'We take only the clothes we stand up in, except for a few pairs of socks and of course they're never removed the whole time, in fact several of them are sown on to save buttons etc. The wolfskin mits are fine things and putting all these things on in the warm hut one wonders how any cold can penetrate them. The finneskoe are also very comfortable, while the sledging wind clothes are so light they feel like a handkerchief.'

The expedition had been suggested by Deb's former tutor, Professor Edgeworth David, in order to re-examine the Royal Society Range that had first been explored by David and Priestley on Shackleton's *Nimrod* Expedition. Accordingly, the Western Party set out on 24 January and headed for the Ferrar and Koettlitz glaciers and the Dry Valleys (largely devoid of snow and ice), examining also the adjacent Suess, Blue and Garwood confluence glaciers. Deb was able to collect specimens of gneisses, marbles and other crystalline rocks along with basalts and kenyte boulders (a form of lava) from nunataks above the glacier surfaces and from surrounding rock outcrops. They had their first contact with Emperor penguins on Ferrar Glacier and Deb described them as '80 lb [36.3 kg] average weight, 3 ft [0.9 m] high, very solid, with the weight low down, so that they easily bob up if knocked down'. His diaries show that he was enjoying this extended camping trip: 'the welcome hiss of the primus stove, the warmth of his sleeping bag and finneskoes and the cosiness of the four-man tent.' Taff Evans kept them amused in the tent by his yarns of former expeditions and his naval adventures. The party reached Shackleton's hut on 14 March on their return, only to find that the depot-laying party had got there on 5 March, making 16 all told in the hut and something of a squeeze. Capt. Scott and most of the hut's occupants left for Cape Evans in early April, and after some delays by blizzard conditions reached base hut by Good Friday, 14 April.

From April to November is the austral winter, and the sun rose for the last time on the 24 April. Deb took advantage of what light there was and had an attempt at a plane-table survey of the district, taking his instruments over to Inaccessible Island, his topographic map being almost completed. He was pleased with the result:

'It has surprised some of our surveying men who have hitherto much looked down upon the plane-table as a surveying instrument. As I have done the whole thing in less than six hours and have got a lot of detail in, while Teddy Evans has hardly half done his, it has naturally surprised them. But of course the accuracy of my map leaves much to be desired.'

Apart from the daily chores of feeding the ponies and reading the meteorological instruments, there was now time to catch up with diaries and to discuss the progress of the expedition. Deb wrote:

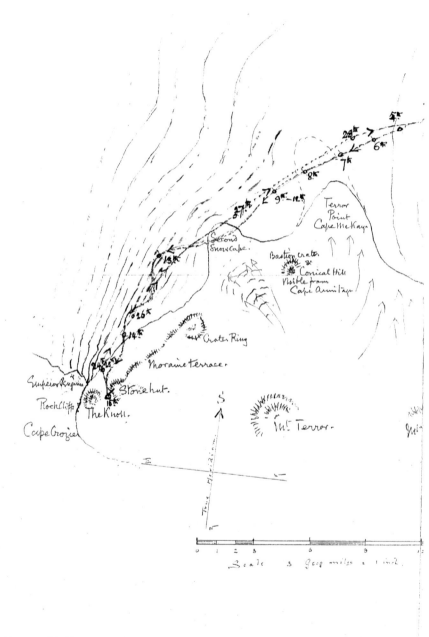

Deb's original field survey of the journey from Cape Evans to Cape Crozier (SPRI)

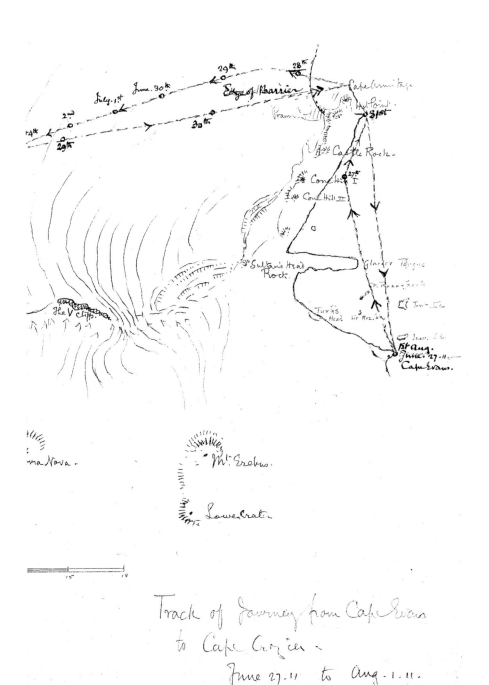

Track of Journey from Cape Evans
to Cape Crozier.
June 27.11 to Aug. 1.11.

'We were discussing Amundsen's chances today, opinions very varied, I think myself that their chances are rather better than ours. To begin with they are 60 miles further south than we are and can make due south at once, whereas we have to dodge round islands. It will need very careful organisation on our side next year. If the Owner [Capt. Scott] will consult the senior men I think it can be done but if he keeps them in the dark as they were on this Depot trip things are likely to go wrong.'

Deb had a similar argument with Birdie on the ethics of Amundsen's attempt for the Pole:

'We both agree that he is entirely unscrupulous and has little or no excuse, but I maintain – while Birdie contradicts – that he at least is taking a lot of risks both physical and moral and that it is a brave venture even if it is unsportsmanlike. Birdie also thinks he has no chance of getting to the Pole. I must say I think he has, if anything, got a better chance than we have.' (Deb's diary, quoted in Debenham Back, 1992: 101)

Poor Birdie – he was destined to be the first to see the Norwegian flag fluttering at the Pole on Amundsen's tent, while Scott and the others were half a day's march away.

When conditions allowed, there would be football matches on the ice outside the hut, and Scott introduced evening lectures three times a week. On 8 May, Scott outlined his 'Future plans of the Expedition', which were more or less adhered to when the final assault was launched. It was on this occasion that Scott revealed his strategy of travel that was to prove such a controversy. Deb records: 'He [Scott] considered to be unsure to assume that the ponies and dogs would be able to help after the bottom of the Beardmore Glacier was reached, and that men alone must be counted upon in the last 2 stages.' Scott would divide the final parties into three units of either three or four men. He maintained that he was frankly disappointed in the dogs and he doubted whether they would get as far as the Beardmore. Also placed no reliance on the motors, though he would send them off a week earlier to show if they would be of any use. He decided that all should take skis to the base of the glacier 'as he thought they would be very useful on the home [run] when the weights were light' (Debenham, Journal III: 38).

Scott later had a private word with Deb. He said that the Pole Party would have to travel so swiftly that there would be no room for a geologist, therefore this ruled out Griffith Taylor, who would retain his position, amongst the remainder, as chief geologist. Although this meant that Deb would not have charge of his own geological party, he realised the logic of his position. Later Deb was to lead a geological expedition in the climb of Mt. Erebus, and so realised a position of authority if only for a period of about one month.

Scott was not a trained scientist, having spent his professional life in the Royal Navy, though in his training he had come first in the examinations for seamanship, and more recently in torpedo management. Nonetheless he was committed to a thorough scientific examination of this part of Antarctica and used the evening lectures as an introduction to the scientific specialisms of his staff. He usually made notes and often asked probing questions. Deb's first lecture was on 'General Principles of Geology', and one not likely to stir the interests of most of the audience, several of whom were seen to nod off to sleep, whilst Atch, Birdie and Soldier clapped at everything and made fun of the specimens. His second lecture 'Volcanoes' was more closely focussed, and obviously relevant in their Cape Evans surroundings (an account of the lecture is given in Jones, 2005: 225–6) II. Scott wrote in his diary: 'His matter is good, but his voice a little monotonous, so that there were signs of slumber in the audience, but all woke up for a warm and amusing discussion succeeding the lecture.' Scott continued that 'Discussion of such a subject sorts out one's ideas.' Deb was still unaccustomed to this sort of lecture, albeit in his later academic life he was renowned for the liveliness of his lectures and the amusing asides. Scott made two pages of notes, which were published posthumously, in his official account of the expedition, and even today might well be included in a textbook of geology. Silas, looking back to his time as physicist on the expedition, wrote in a letter to Reginald Pound: 'despite his very considerable interest in our scientific activities, Scott had a difficulty in understanding the mental make-up of scientists . . . ', and yet 'He could analyse statements and theories in a very embarrassing manner' (Pound, 1968: 241). Pound asserts: 'What none in the Expedition knew (and few thereafter) was how closely he was observing their individual performances, and assessing them as likely supporters of his final effort to reach the Pole.' For a later evening lecture, Deb chose a topic with wider appeal – 'Bushcraft in the Australian Outback'!

Scott in his personal journals was candid in his comments, no matter what he might say with his staff. For instance, of Simpson he observed:

> 'Admirable as a worker, admirable as a scientist, admirable as a lecturer, but irritating as a companion. Irritation caused by want of worldly wisdom and not at all through lack of good nature, its manifestation occasioned by the display of cocksureness and by unconscious facial expression . . . His is an example of a manner to be avoided, but he wouldn't be grateful to be told so.'

He set the qualities of Griffith Taylor against those of his fellow geologist Debenham:

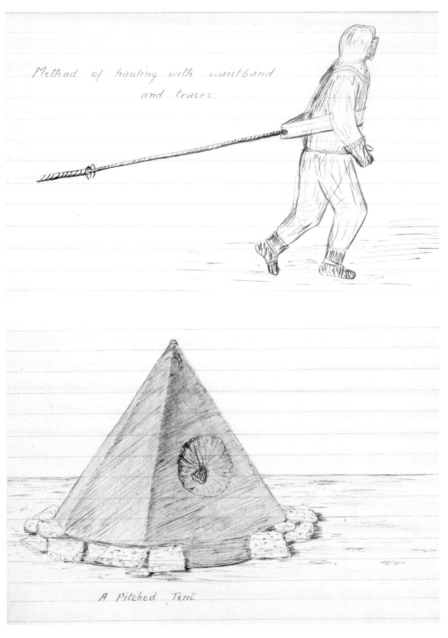

Sketches from Deb's Antarctic diary (SPRI)

'Taylor's intellect is omnivorous and versatile, his mind unceasingly active, his grasp wide. Yet on a different plane he strikes doubt. Will he just fail to stamp his work with originality? I confess a difficulty to grasp his full meaning to the Expedition. Debenham is clearer. Here we have a well-trained sturdy worker who realises the conception of thoroughness, conscientiousness but not brilliancy.' (Pound, 1968: 242)

Of the other member of the Western Party, Silas, Scott wrote: 'his mind saturated with the ice problems of this wonderful region, was a good-hearted, strong and keen, a hard and conscientious worker who has an excellent knowledge of physics, but not a great aptitude for applying that knowledge' (Pound, 1968: 241–2). On the other hand, he wrote of Birdie:

'Little Bowers remains a marvel . . . he is thoroughly enjoying himself. I leave all the provisions in his hands, and at all times he knows how we stand, or how each returning party should fare . . . Nothing comes amiss to him, and no work is too hard. It is difficult to get him into the tent; he seems quite oblivious of the cold, and he lies coiled in his bag writing and working out sights long after the others are asleep.' (Jones, 2005: 369–70).

On 24 April the sun rose for the last time and the explorers had to face the dark southern winter, accommodated in their hut at Cape Evans, and plan for the next season's expeditions, including the attempt on the South Pole. Apart from the daily routine of making outside meteorological measurements, and the gravity and magnetic readings, the work was principally in the shelter of the hut, or close by feeding the horses and dogs, checking and preparing tents, sledges and clothing for the next expeditions. The two doctors, Wilson and Atkinson, started a monthly set of measurements of the physique of all personnel. Deb records his height at 5 ft 8 in (1.72 m), chest 38 in (1.15 m) and weight 11 st 2 lb (70.7 kg).

Ponting spent many hours developing and printing his negatives, and Deb produced some excellent prints of the sledging of the Western Party. Wilson perfected his own watercolour sketches and assisted any others who wanted to paint, and Cherry-Garrard edited the *South Polar Times*. At this time the daily routine was casual and easy. Unless Deb was taking his turn as night watchman, he would rise at 7.30 a.m. with the others, complete his ablutions – at least twice a week by rubbing himself all over in snow – and be at breakfast between 8.00 and 8.30 a.m. This meal consisted of porridge, tea or coffee, bread and butter, fried seal or bacon, or scrambled 'Tru-egg', all prepared by the cook, Clissold. This would be followed by Deb working at his geological specimens or developing film in the dark room. Lunch would be at 1.00 p.m., of soup with bread or biscuit and butter, potted meat, jam and cheese and, on alternate days, tea or cocoa. The afternoon was often spent reading from the considerable library until supper at 6.00 p.m., of soup followed by a meat course and a pudding. On special days, such as birthdays or days of national celebration, wines would be served, followed by liqueurs. Then Cherry, who had contributed £1,000 towards the expedition and hence had a degree of independence, would bring out some of his private provisions like fruit cake and almonds or raisins (Debenham, Journal III: 31). The three-times-a-week evening lectures would be maintained by a roster of scientists and officers. In the strong tradition of naval practices, the usual Sunday services were continued with virtually full attendances.

Although the sun was now absent, there was often sufficient moonlight for games of football to be played on the nearby snow- and ice-covered surface, and this was a welcome and lively diversion from the otherwise monotonous daily grind. Debenham was a frequent player, although he had little knowledge of the rules, having been a rugby player at school. On 2 May he records in his diary (Journal III: 29): 'Played football – Gran and Soldier were the respective captains. Association was played.' Deb was frequently penalised for handling the ball as he was not familiar with the rules of Association Football. The temperature was –10, and a blizzard blew up in the second half to the advantage of the other side, and Deb's team was beaten three goals to nil. Atch turned out to be the best player. They played nine a side and had no referee. The Russian groom Anton Omelchenko, a former jockey, was puzzled throughout, and not sure which side he was on until the end of the game. A return match was held the following day and Deb's side restored some credibility by losing only four goals to five. Deb collided with the 14 st 6 lb bulk of Taff Evans during the match, and returned to the hut very sore and had difficulty getting into his bunk.

Deb commented on the lack of musical expertise amongst the expedition shore party, which numbered 32 in total. Deb played his flute only occasionally, Nelson had a mandolin but it was hardly used, and the pianola, which required just constant pedalling, was practised, but only by a few. Deb complained that Bill played the pieces in stately adagio, when allegretto would have been more appropriate, and Gran was much too heavy, 'pedal fortissimo is his method throughout'. Otherwise it was the wind-up gramophone that formed the musical entertainment, 'for no-one can really play the piano, and no-one sings'.

Midwinter Day, 22 June, was celebrated by the publication of the first edition of the *South Polar Times*, and a special meal was served in the evening, followed by a round of speeches called for by Capt. Scott. The Norwegian, Tryggve Gran, found himself in a somewhat invidious position; Gran spoke of Amundsen, and his own peculiar position on an English expedition competing with a Norwegian one. But he said that he was committed to this one and not only sorry that the Norwegian had come but that, from the depth of his heart, he wished Capt. Scott success in the fight. Deb kept to safer ground by speaking of the natural pride that Australia would take in the expedition.

Then a 'Christmas tree' was brought in, made by Birdie Bowers from an old ski stick with streamers, flaming candles and crackers. Presents, which had been prepared by Miss Souper, Wilson's sister-in-law, were distributed to all. Then the table was removed and a set of lancers performed.

One major event in this period was the famous excursion by Wilson, Bowers and Cherry-Garrard to Cape Crozier in search of Emperor penguin eggs. They left on 27 June 1911 in the darkness of the austral winter and returned, exhausted, on 8 August after enduring some of the harshest polar conditions on record. For most of the time they were facing blizzards with the temperature reaching at times 109 degrees of frost. The wind was so strong that it removed the tented cover of their shelter, and it was only discovered by luck; Cherry, who was desperately shortsighted, had to struggle along for most of the time with no sense of direction. This winter journey subsequently gave rise to one of the great classics of all polar literature, *The Worst Journey in the World* by Apsley Cherry-Garrard (1922).

From the middle of August daylight was noticeably increasing, ponies and dogs were exercised, and final preparations made for the Southern Party, that is, the assault on the Pole. First contingents of the supporting group, the motor sledges, were away by 24 October and the others soon afterwards. Deb knew, from Scott, that he was not to be included in the final small party destined for the Pole, and he had been excluded also from the support parties as, together with Griff and Priestley, he had been despatched to geologise in the region of Granite Harbour.

The party to explore the coast of Victoria Land as far north as Granite Harbour comprised Deb, Griff (leader), Gran and seaman Forde. They left Cape Evans on 14 November after the Pole Party had already gone. The object was to survey the area around Granite Harbour and the Mackay glacier tongue, and to remain there until relieved by *Terra Nova*, under Capt. Pennell.

Deb continued his plane-table surveying and Griff fixed topographic points by theodolite. They pitched a permanent camp just west of Discovery Bluff, named it Camp Geology, and from there sledged across the glacier and on to the Devil's Punchbowl. Griff and Deb were collecting rock specimens from outcrops and glacier moraines. They found examples of Beacon sandstone, marbles, tremolite and other minerals. Deb discovered a specimen of brown coal amongst the shales, and a number of fossils. These were bagged and found their way ultimately to Cambridge for further examination. Forde spent his spare hours in hunting for seals to add to the food supply. They were supposed to be relieved on 15 January, but there was no sign of the ship. On 15 February Gran spotted the smoke of *Terra Nova* out beyond the ice edge, and with difficulty the geological party embarked, but did not get back at Cape Evans until 26 February.

Then *Terra Nova* turned back to pick up Teddy Evans, Lashly and Silas and to deliver them also to Cape Evans, and to pack on board everything and everyone who was going home. On the way they hoped to have a second attempt at locating Victor

Campbell and the Northern Party, but ice conditions and visibility made this impossible. The ship returned to New Zealand on 5 March, leaving Deb and his fellow explorers for another winter. Ponting had gone back, so Deb was now the official photographer.

As the southern summer sun began to fade, anxiety rose amongst those now in the hut at Cape Evans over the fate of both Capt. Scott and the Pole Party, and Victor Campbell and the Northern Party. Their calculations showed that, if all had gone well, the Pole Party should have returned to One Ton Depot on 12 March and Corner Camp on 23 March. By 28 April, Deb and the others were giving up any hope of survival of their comrades: 'So it seems useless to hope any longer but whilst I cannot give up yet, we must face the fact that we have lost our five strongest men, and four of them seniors and born leaders', wrote Deb in his journal.

As far as Campbell was concerned, Deb was more optimistic: 'I can't imagine that the ship did not eventually pick up Campbell so they are there somewhere. I think they must have decided to winter there probably because they found travelling along the coast impossible until too late to start.'

The Northern Party, under the leadership of Campbell, had started from Cape Evans on the *Terra Nova* on 27 January 1911 to sail along the ice edge of McMurdo Bay. They first encountered Amundsen at Framheim and spent a brief, pleasant, if somewhat uncomfortable time with the Norwegians, and then turned back to disembark at Cape Adare on 18 February. The other members of the party were Surgeon George Murray Levick, Raymond Priestley, Petty Officers George Abbott and Frank Browning, and Seaman Harry Dickason. Their objective was to study the geology and glaciology of part of South Victoria Land, to compile detailed maps of the Barrier ice in this area, record the frequency of the aurora, make meticulous recordings of the meteorology, and to collect large hauls of specimens of rocks, fossils and plants (mosses and lichens). The strategy was for *Terra Nova* to pick them up on 15 March at the latest, and to return them to Cape Evans, but the ship was unable, because of the ice conditions, to moor anywhere near enough for them to signal their position. The six explorers were destined to spend virtually a whole year in this region, spending the bitterly cold, sunless winter in an ice cave with diminishing food supplies. Eventually they were able to start sledging from Terra Nova Bay for home, stumbling across a cache of food left for emergencies, and arrived at Hut Point where there was warmth, shelter and plenty of rations. After a thankful stay in the hut they set off for the base hut at Cape Evans, arriving there on 7 November to find the hut empty, but soon Deb and Archer returned, to welcome baths and a sumptuous meal. The account of Victor Campbell's northern expedition deserves to rank alongside the journeys taken by Wilson, Cherry-Garrard and Bowers and the final polar odyssey of Capt. Scott and his four immortal companions.

In the absence of Scott, the leadership of the remaining members of the Shore Party was taken by Campbell. Whilst all were waiting for news of Scott, Campbell

gave permission for Deb, Priestley and Dickason to continue with mapping and geol-
ogising as soon as the weather improved. Their choice was an ascent of the 12,400 ft
(3,799 m) Mt. Erebus, the smoking volcano that was visible from Cape Evans whenever the clouds cleared.

Deb was anxious to follow in the footsteps of Edgeworth David – his university
professor who had climbed Mt. Erebus in 1908 – to extend the maps of the Erebus
massif and to add to the collection of rocks and fossils. Campbell made Deb the
leader of this trip, although he was nominally junior to Priestley. A date at the end
of November was set for the start of the expedition, but it was 2 December before
they departed. The group consisted of Deb, Priestley, Gran, Dickason, Hooper and
Abbott.

Deb and his party sledged to Cape Royds and pitched tents on the old moraine
above it. The climbing party split into two, with Deb and Abbott initially mapping
with the plane-table and theodolite, whilst Priestley with Gran, Hooper and
Dickason went ahead collecting rocks, mainly volcanic tuffs, as they climbed. At
Camp E, 8,000 ft (243.8 m) up the mountain, all were feeling the effects of altitude
sickness, but Deb and Dickason (both heavy smokers) were worse affected. Priestley
and the others reached first the rim of a parasitic cone and were later joined by Deb,
but when Priestley's party continued up the steep, icy slope, Deb and Dickason were
unable to keep going and spent the time photographing, mapping and collecting. By
15 December they had all returned to the Cape Royds Hut, where they found
Campbell, Cherry, Atch, Silas, Williamson and Archer, who had sledged over from
Cape Evans. Deb's party then stayed at Cape Royds until the end of the month, living
on the splendid food cache that had been left behind by Shackleton's expedition;
amongst other delicacies there were sardines, ptarmigan, blackcock, bottled fruits,
cakes in tins, plum puddings, jams and so on, and all in abundance. On Boxing Day
they spread themselves with a real festival feast. They had also a good haul of rocks,
about 80 lb apiece, which were cached to be recovered later when *Terra Nova* had
been sighted.

Deb was vindicated in his assumption that Campbell's party would survive the
dreadful winter in Queen Victoria Land, and his worst fears over the Pole Party were
realised when the three-dog party members amongst those searching for Scott and
his companions returned to Cape Evans on 25 November. These were surgeon
Atkinson, Cherry-Garrard and Demetri. Deb's reaction, in the words of his own
diary, records the grief felt by all who participated in the *Terra Nova* Expedition. If the
words seem familiar, it should be remembered that Deb had listened with the others
in silence as the last entries in the journals and diaries of Scott, Wilson and Bowers
were read out in base camp. He wrote:

'Briefly thus: 11 miles beyond 79° 30' depot (One Ton Depot) they saw
the peak of a tent showing, and knew the object of their search was

attained. It was right on course and as I say only 11 miles off a fully
stocked depot. In the tent were the bodies of Bill, Birdie, and the
Owner, dead of cold, hunger, and fatigue. All the records were with them
and everything possible is known.'

They had reached the South Pole on 17 January to find that the Norwegians had
reached it just one month earlier.

On the journey down the glacier, Taff Evans – already a little weak – had a bad
fall and got concussion. At the bottom of the glacier he failed and died before they
reached the depot. Awful temperatures, wretched surface and lateness in reaching
depots made them all weak, and Soldier failed next. He knew he was delaying them
and in one blizzard walked out and away and he was never seen again. He did it inten-
tionally, to save his comrades – a fitting death for a real hero.

The other three marched on to 79° 41' and reached it on 21 March, with just
enough oil and food to reach One Ton Depot. But then came a nine-day blizzard
during which they gradually weakened, and the last entry in the Owner's diary was
on 29 March: 'I cannot write more of it now, it is rather overwhelming at first'
(Debenham, Journal III: 147).

The tragedy of the deaths of Scott, Wilson, Bowers, Edgar Evans and Oates, in the
harshest of environments and for so many months, was felt by all members of the
expedition; most grievously, because these men had died on their return after reaching the South Pole but without gaining priority, as the Norwegians had beaten them
to this coveted prize by about one month. It gave the assault on the Pole some of the
elements of a Greek tragedy, a metaphor not lost on Deb with his first degree in
Classics. The bodies of the dead comrades were eventually discovered on the Barrier
Ice and their personal belongings removed. Those back at base, Camp Evans, continued the scientific work, but ultimately all the remaining members of Scott's expedition party were ready to leave for home.

January 1913 was spent mainly in packing stores, expedition records, as well as
personal items for return to home. The smoke of the ship was first spotted off Cape
Royds on 18 January, and they all left Cape Evans on 23 January. *Terra Nova* headed
first for Cape Royds to collect the rocks depoted at the Hut, and then made fast on
the ice edge. It was a very different occasion from their arrival in McMurdo Sound
on 4 January 1911: then an enthusiastic company were anticipating a successful assault
on the South Pole, and now they must face the rest of the world with the news of
the deaths of five brave men. The aim of the expedition had been achieved, the Pole
had been reached – but at what a price! The attempt could be seen as a glorious
failure. As Capt. Scott had said in his farewell message: 'Had we lived, I should have
had a tale to tell of the hardiness, endurance, and courage of my companions which
would have stirred the heart of every Englishman'. Those crossing the Southern
Ocean at that time, bound for New Zealand and Australia, could have had no idea of

the effects that Scott's last message was to have on a expectant world, nor of the volu-minous accounts, analyses and criticisms it would generate.

One of Deb's last acts onshore was to carry, on 18 January, an immense cross of Australian jarrah wood to erect on Observation Hill overlooking the Barrier Ice. The shore party of Atch, Cherry, Silas and Deb, together with four seamen, carried by sledge the 12 ft (3.65 m) cross that had been prepared by the ship's carpenter as a permanent memorial to Scott and the others, whose bodies were to be left behind. They trudged across nine miles (14.48 km) of snow and ice to Observation Hill, where the cross was erected overlooking the Ross Ice Shelf. The inscription read:

IN MEMORIAM
CAPT. SCOTT, R.N.
Dr E. A. WILSON, CAPT. L. E. G. OATES, INSK. DGS.,
LIEUT. H. R. BOWERS, R.I.M.
PETTY OFFFICER EDGAR EVANS, R.N.
WHO DIED ON THEIR RETURN
FROM
THE POLE
MARCH 1912

Below the names was the simple tribute, taken from Tennyson's Ulysses:

'To strive, to seek, to find, and not to yield.'

Cdr. Teddy Evans, second in command to Capt. Scott, who had assumed the overall responsibility for the expedition, appointed a small committee to help in the final arrangements for the disposal of the expedition's records. It was this responsibil-ity that would bring him to England and to Cambridge.

The ship carried the remaining ponies and dogs and some of the removable stores; the rest were left in the hut at Cape Evans. Deb brought back, for himself, one of the older dogs, Tresor.

The ship and the remaining company finally left Antarctica on 19 January 1913. Cdr. Teddy Evans now took control of plans for the future. At a meeting of all scien-tists and officers in the wardroom on 27 January, he officially gave complete custody of the geological specimens and the photographic apparatus and records to Frank Debenham. Deb was required to write up the geological records and to conserve the photographic materials. All the scientific results were to be worked out in England. This, by itself was sufficient to impel Debenham to England, and he spent only a short time with family and friends in Australia before setting out for Cambridge.

Although he was quite unaware of its significance at the time, Cambridge was destined to be the place where Deb's greatest academic achievements would be realised in the formation of the University Department of Geography, and the creation of the Scott Polar Research Institute. Cambridge would continue to play a seminal part in polar studies and polar exploration. It became an attraction for all those involved in the scientific investigation of the polar world and a scholarly meeting place for former polar explorers. The last of the members of Scott's 1910–13 expedition to come to Cambridge was the veteran Norwegian Tryggve Gran, who entertained the Friends of the SPRI with his Antarctic experiences one Saturday evening in October 1974. He had earlier that month given a lecture at the Royal Geographical Society in London. He died in Norway on 8 January 1980, aged 90; he was the last of all the scientific shore party from *Terra Nova* (Stonehouse, 1980–81: 180).

The practice of leaving caches of personal belongings and equipment in the field, away from the principal bases, has led to unexpected finds at later – sometimes much later – times. When Ann Shirley, archivist of SPRI, was in New Zealand in 1957, explorers from that country found perfectly preserved relics of Capt. Scott's 1912 expedition at Cape Roberts, some 100 miles north of Scott Base in McMurdo Sound. The items discovered included clothing, a film changing bag, and a small kit-bag marked with the name of Frank Debenham. Deb wrote to Ann on 18 October 1957 saying that five newspapers had telephoned asking what was in the bag, to which he had replied 'Sorry, I've forgotten'. He really thought it was a singlet he wore continuously for four months, 'so it will stand up for itself'!

In 1963 Deb heard from an American expedition which had retrieved a book left from a sledging expedition in 1912. It was *Tales of Mystery and Imagination* by Edgar Allan Poe, buried under a sealskin, with a sledge on top. Apart from a little water damage around the edges, it was in a better condition than two similar copies bought in 1961 in Manchester, where Deb sent it to be tested. Dr Hudson of Manchester College of Science and Technology said, 'natural wastage can be slowed by cold storage' (*Daily Telegraph*, 1965).

CHAPTER 3

Geography and the University of Cambridge

As a discrete discipline of study, Geography is a relative newcomer to the curricula of British universities. It was first offered in 1888 when, in midsummer, the University of Cambridge appointed Francis Henry Hill Guillemard (1852–1933) as a lecturer for five years. Although his tenure of the lectureship actually lasted only six months, his appointment was of some significance to Frank Debenham, who came on the University scene some 30 years later.

Guillemard spent much of his early life travelling in Europe, and then joined an expedition to South Africa; between 1882 and 1884 he extended his geographical knowledge by serving as naturalist on the *Marchesa*, visiting the Far East from Kamchatka in the North Pacific to Japan, Borneo and New Guinea. Virtually all his later life was spent in Cambridge, residing after 1898 at the Old Mill House, Trumpington, just to the south of Cambridge. He became a well-known Cambridge eccentric, but retained his interest in the teaching of geography and was a member of the first Board of Geographical Studies, which met in 1904, serving for some years without a break, and attending meetings thereafter until the end of 1922 (Stoddart, 1986: 95, footnote). The other members of the Board were: Professor George Darwin, Dr J.E. Marr (Geology), Dr J.B. Bury (representing history and archaeology), Dr A.W. Ward (of the board of economics and politics), Sir Clements Markham and Dr John S. Keltie (representing the Royal Geographical Society), the Vice-Chancellor, and Frank Debenham, the Reader in Geography.

Guillemard donated considerable collections of photographs and paintings of Africa to both the Royal Geographical Society (RGS, or 'the Society') and to the embryonic Scott Polar Research Institute (SPRI, or 'the Institute'). He became General Editor of the *Cambridge County Geographies* series, for use in schools, utilis-ing his contacts with members of the University to write the various county volumes. Thus the authors of the volume on Cambridgeshire, published in 1909, were the Woodwardian Professor of Geology, T. McKenny Hughes and his wife, Mary Caroline Hughes. After Deb's appointment as lecturer in geography in 1919, he kept in touch with Guillemard, who, like Deb, was also a Fellow of Gonville and Caius College.

The establishment of geography as a subject available to undergraduates in Cambridge University was prolonged by the reluctance of many members of the

Senate to acknowledge its value, alongside the traditional subjects of Classics, philosophy and mathematics. Its relevance to contemporary studies was urged by others, particularly the natural scientists whose subject curricula had only recently been accepted at that time. Compelling reasons for the inclusion of geography in the University's calendar of lectures were provided by arguments set forth by a number of Royal Commissions, and by sustained pressure from the RGS, which by the mid-nineteenth century was calling for a revision of the teaching of geography in schools and the universities. The RGS looked to the universities of Oxford and Cambridge to take a lead, appoint professors and set up departments of geography.

The lobbying of these venerable institutions has been admirably researched by Dr David Ross Stoddart (1975, 1986) and by the late Professor Edmund Gilbert (1971).

In 1850 a Royal Commission was appointed to enquire into the condition, studies and revenues of Cambridge University. This Commission reported in 1852. Whilst there was no specific brief to consider geography per se, the commissioners argued for some teaching of a geographical nature, more from social than from academic and scholarly considerations:

'. . . there is a very important class of Students who resort to the Universities with no professional views, and who, from their expectations in life, have no motive for prosecuting the severe studies beyond the prescribed minimum . . . This is a class which it is in every way desirable to induce to the University, and to influence for good when there.

Many of this class of Students become travellers, to whom a knowledge of natural science, and a familiarity with many scientific processes and the handling of a great variety of instruments are likely to be of eminent use, and to whom the example of Humboldt may stimulate to bring home records of more importance than the usual reminiscences of travellers for pleasure. The theory, handling, and systematic use of meteorological and magnetic instruments are an element of the scientific education of a traveller of the last importance; a practical acquaintance with photography not less so.' (Royal Commission, 1852: 118–19, quoted by Stoddart, 1975)

Although this recommendation was a long time before it was in any way implemented, it prefaced many of Deb's ideas 60 years later. He would endorse the emphasis on observation, instrumentation and systematic scientific analysis inherent in the commission's argument. Moreover, at that time there were many members of the University, particularly in the departments of the natural sciences, who would endorse these views, notably Professor Alfred Newton, who held the first chair in zoology.

On 3 July 1871 the RGS addressed a memorandum to the Vice-Chancellors of both Oxford and Cambridge Universities on the subject of geography in education:

'We would point out the special importance of geography to Englishmen in the present age. The possession of great and widely scattered dependencies, the unprecedented extension of our commercial interests, the increased freedom of intercourse and closeness of connections abolished by means of the steamship and the telegraph, between our country and all parts of the world, the progress of emigration binding us by ties of blood relationship to so many distant communities – all these are circumstances which vastly enhance the value of geographical knowledge . . .'

This urged a 'practical and commonsense Victorian attitude to the subject' (Gilbert, 1971) and continued:

'We speak of geography, not as a barren catalogue of names and facts, but as a science that ought to be taught in a liberal way, with abundant appliances of maps, models, and illustrations . . . We look to the Universities, not only to rescue geography from being badly taught in the schools of England, but to raise it to an even higher standard than it has yet attained.'

This quotation of the 1871 memorandum comes from a Report to the RGS by John Scott Keltie (1886), who had been appointed the Society's Inspector of Geographical Education in 1885. His brief was to examine the teaching of the subject in both the universities and in the schools. He recalled in his Report that the Society had recommended to the Royal Commissioners the 'establishment of Geographical Professorships' at both Oxford and Cambridge, and reminded the commissioners that professorships in the subject were already appointed in many of the universities of France and Germany.

On 14 March 1887 a select committee appointed by the University, consisting of senior members of the University and representatives of the RGS, submitted their report on the teaching of geography, proposing a lectureship for five years, at a stipend composed of £50 a year from the University and £150 from the RGS. There was an expected opposition from those members of the Senate who regarded the subject as not a science, and without the intellectual rigour of a university discipline. The leading protagonist was Alfred Newton, who declared:

'Whether it was an Art or a Science he did not much care. It was a study to be seriously pursued, but until something was done in the way of encouraging it in the University, he believed that the present ignorance of geography among so-called educated people would continue.' (quoted in Stoddart, 1975: 223)

Following the brief tenure of Guillemard as lecturer, the post was advertised for a five-year appointment. There seems to have been some approach to persuade Hugh Robert Mill to apply (see Stoddart, 1975: 224), but on 23 May 1889 it was confirmed that a Scotsman, John Young Buchanan, had accepted the position. He was a person of considerable wealth, and had made his reputation as physicist and chemist on the voyage of the *Challenger*, the first major scientific circumnavigation of the world. He had investigated sea temperatures on the surface and at depth, and prepared maps of oceanic salinity. He was later knighted, elected a Fellow of Christ's College in Cambridge, and maintained a private yacht, laboratories in Edinburgh and London, and sailed with the Prince of Monaco to Spitsbergen on *Princesse Alice*, the finest oceanographic vessel of its day. He was a principal supporter of the *Scotia* Expedition to the South Orkneys and the Weddell Sea led by William Speirs Bruce between 1902 and 1904. He gave his lectures, mainly on scientific aspects of geography, in rooms in the Sedgwick Building of the New Museums site off Downing Street, Cambridge. His period of office came to an end in 1893 and the post was re-advertised. Throughout these early days of the lectureship in geography, the RGS maintained a financial contribution to the salary of the stipend of £150 per year, with £50 from the university. This financial support from the RGS continued until 1923, by which time the first honours students were graduating.

The next holder of this post was H. Yule Oldham, who had graduated with a BA from Oxford in 1886. He was appointed on 8 June 1893, and his tenure of the post lasted 28 years. He was primarily interested in education and had taught in several schools including Harrow and Hulme Grammar School, Manchester, as well as in the University of Berlin and Owens College, Manchester. He also gave many extension lectures in the principal towns and cities of northern England and the Midlands. He offered courses on general geography, physical geography and the geography of central Europe. In 1898 Oldham's post was elevated to that of the RGS Readership in Geography. He continued with his lecture courses, which could be supplemented by a practical course in map-making and map-reading for an extra fee of one guinea. For a further three guineas, courses in the Lent Term of 1903 were offered. These were given by lecturers from cognate disciplines: A.C. Haddon, anthropology and ethnology; J.E. Marr, geomorphology and geology; E.J. Garwood, plane-table and photographic surveying; and A.R. Hinks, elementary astronomical surveying. These special lectures were advertised as suitable for those 'who wish to undertake exploration, or who, while travelling or being stationed in foreign countries desire to contribute to our knowledge about them.' This spectrum of courses, particularly after the appointment of Philip Lake in 1908 as lecturer in physical geography, became for some four decades the basis of teaching in the Cambridge Department of Geography.

This specialist interest in physical geography and surveying produced a significant difference between what was taught in Cambridge and what was emphasised in Oxford. A Readership at Oxford, with the help of the RGS, had been established earlier, in 1887, and Halford John Mackinder had been appointed. He had that same year delivered his seminal paper on 'Scope and methods of geography' (Mackinder, 1887: 141–60), and begun a tradition of the study of regional, economic and political geography which was to be continued by Andrew John Herbertson and others into the 1950s. Herbertson became the first Professor of Geography at Oxford in 1904, 27 years before Frank Debenham became the first Professor of Geography at Cambridge.

The Board of Geographical Studies in Cambridge, constituted in February 1904, regulated the lecture courses and agreed the regulations for the special examination and the diploma in geography. The first examinations took place in the Corn Exchange in May and June 1907. As yet there was no examination for an honours degree in geography. A small library was organised for the subject and a subscription taken with the *Geographical Journal*, and a small equipment store was provided. Between 1907–1908 a serious controversy arose within the Board on the continuing support by the RGS of the readership and the competence of Yule Oldham. At times this became quite acrimonious and was advanced vehemently by Clements Markham, a former Secretary and recently past President of the RGS. The matter was resolved by Yule Oldham resigning the readership, but continuing to hold a lecture-

James Wordie and Frank Debenham, group photograph of the Sedgwick Club, 1920 (Earth Sciences)

ship alongside two new appointments: Philip Lake in physical and economic geography, and Arthur Hinks as the RGS lecturer in surveying and cartography. The RGS grant continued and a new nominee was sought to replace Clements Markham on the Board (see Stoddart, 1986: 109–122). By the time Deb arrived in Cambridge, geography was well established in the University; in 1913–14 there were 32 students taking Part One, and 18 taking Part Two. The significance of the RGS in the early history of the Department of Geography at Cambridge can be measured by their financial contribution – amounting to £7,250 in the 35 years ending in 1923.

When Deb arrived in Cambridge from the Antarctic he was accepted at once as a member by Gonville and Caius College. He naturally moved towards the Sedgwick Museum and the Department of Geology, and he was given the use of attic rooms to sort and identify the rocks and fossils that he had brought back from the *Terra Nova* Expedition. He had also been given the task of completing those maps and surveys that had been drafted at Cape Evans. Before this could in any way be finished, the Great War had been declared and Deb volunteered and was recruited, for the whole of the war, into the 7th Battalion of Oxford and Bucks. Light Infantry. On his return to Cambridge he was admitted to the degree of BA in 1919, and was elected to a fellowship of Gonville and Caius. In the same year he was honoured for his war service by the award of CBE (Military). He returned to his commitment to the Antarctic expedition records and worked on the *Report on Geology*, co-authored with Griffith Taylor (1964). At this time he was married with a young daughter and required urgently some permanent position in order to improve his financial situation.

Another of the tasks awaiting Deb on his return from war service was the completion of the cartographic and survey reports for the *Terra Nova* Expedition, an important task that Deb had promised Capt. Evans on leaving the Antarctic. Still in his attic rooms in the Sedgwick Buildings, Deb finally put together the sketches, precise surveys, both topographic and hydrographic, and the measured angular and linear measurements. The attic rooms had been loaned to Deb by the Professor of Geology, J.E. Marr; the space was reached by a long, stone, spiral staircase and consisted of a barrel-roofed cavity which ran for the whole length of the L-shaped building. It was ideal for storage. Marr and McKenny Hughes were using it to store unsorted materials for the Geology Museum, and Deb added his Antarctic rocks and fossils in the east end of the attic and soon made it a depository for polar equipment, notably sledges and tents. He brought in drawing tables and cartographic instruments, and it became the infant collection for a 'polar centre'. It was to last in this state from 1913 to 1927 and became a calling station for all who were interested in polar expeditions. (Today the entire space has been divided into laboratories and offices, so there is little now that can be recognised as Deb's first workplace.) In 1927 the University sanctioned a move to the more convenient and quite handsome building of Lensfield House at the corner of Panton Street and Lensfield Road.

The four sledge-mates in Cambridge, November 1913 (SPRI): *standing*, Debenham and Wright; *sitting*, Taylor and Priestley

The official honorary editor of the physical reports of the expedition was originally Col. H.G. Lyons, FRS, appointed by the Mansion House Committee of the
Captain Scott Fund. Lyons had intended to produce a memoir, written by him, with
full reports by various officers concerned with the survey work, but Deb was not very
happy with this decision as Lyons had not been with the expedition, and was somewhat obstructive when Deb questioned him about the data. In a letter dated 12
December 1913, Deb wrote to Cherry: 'I have seen Lyons, he is a blighter'. Lyons had
implied that the survey and cartographic work was dependent on Debenham and his
colleagues. In any case, the cartographic work had originally been in the hands of
Lieut. H. de P. Rennick, RN, assisted by Lieut. H.L. Pennell, who captained the ship
during the survey operations. Both Rennick and Pennell were lost at sea during the
Great War, and much of their preliminary reports were not available. Lyons asked Deb,
in these circumstances, to proceed 'as best as he could'.

Frank Debenham had to redraw, in the Sedgwick attic, many of the maps and
calculate co-ordinate positions. In these matters he was helped in Cambridge by his
former Antarctic colleagues, Wright, Priestley, Campbell and Evans. His *Report on the
Maps and Surveys of the British* (Terra Nova) *Antarctic Expedition, 1910–1913* was
published in London in 1923. It was in the style consistent with the other reports,
and comprises an introductory section explaining the instruments, their method of
use in such a hostile environment where customary surveying practices were not
always possible, and a set of 14 maps provided in a pocket at the back of the report.
This comparatively short report demonstrates the contribution made in field surveying carried out by Deb whilst with Scott, and the validity of his post in the
Geography Department as Lecturer in Cartography and Surveying. His students at
Cambridge felt they were being given lectures and practice by a master of his art.
Gordon Manley has recorded with pride how, when an undergraduate in the early
1920s, he and others were given the task of the re-calculation the position of the
South Pole, originally made by Bowers.

The principal instruments carried in the *Terra Nova* were six theodolites specially
constructed in England by T. Cooke and Sons, the premier manufacturer of surveying instruments at the time, eight chronometers for fixing longitude, six sledgemeters
for distance measurement, twelve aneroids for height fixing, and hypsometers, ther-
mometers and naval sextants. A plane-table was used for the mapping of small areas,
and was particularly favoured by Deb.

The maps are varied in scale and include a map of what was known at that time
of the Antarctic continent, as well as a detailed reconstruction of the route to the
South Pole followed by Capt. Scott and his various parties. On somewhat larger scales
are the details of the Western Journey, Granite Harbour and the ascent of Mt. Erebus.

Arthur Hinks had been appointed to give weekly lectures on surveying from
1903, but resigned his post in July 1913 to become assistant secretary of the RGS,
taking over from J. S. Keltie. Hinks was replaced by Deb's former Antarctic colleague,

Charles Wright, who held the position from January 1914 until 30 September 1916, but in 1915 Wright left for war service and Philip Lake had to deputise for him. Although Wright's appointment had been renewed, in absentia, for five years from 1 October 1916, he resigned when the war ended, and Deb was appointed to the RGS lectureship in surveying and cartography for five years from 1 October 1919. Although Hinks now had a full-time office at the RGS in London, he lived in Royston, not far from Cambridge, and maintained an active interest in the fortunes of geography at Cambridge. He had published two influential works whilst lecturing in Cambridge: *Map Projections* (1912) and *Maps and Survey* (1913), which continued to be used until after the Second World War. So Deb found himself, somewhat fortuitously, in an embryonic Department of Geography, rather than in a well-established and traditional Department of Geology.

Deb discussed his change of lifestyle and his prospects in a lengthy letter to Cherry-Garrard (reproduced in full in Chapter 4). He was clearly much exercised in his plans for the future development of a School of Geography, but his ambitions were two–fold: to provide accommodation for Geography and to allow for research in polar studies as a memorial to the men who died so tragically at the Pole. At the time of writing to Cherry-Garrard, the School of Geography had no permanent home with purpose-built lecture rooms and laboratories. In the early days of the subject, lectures were given in the Department of Chemistry, and then successively in two rooms in the Department of Geology, vacant rooms in Downing Place at the rear of the Baptist Chapel, and ultimately in a building erected for the Department of Forestry. The growing popularity of the subject was clearly impressing on the Senate the need for a new Department of Geography. Cherry-Garrard had replied to Deb's proposals, professing some financial distress over the taxation of wealthy landowners. If Deb had hoped for a promise of substantial funding in that direction, he was disappointed and he wrote again, from 48 Lensfield Road, to Cherry on 2 June 1920:

'I knew that things had been fairly impossible for land owners for some time but imagined that you were getting clear. What I did not realise was the time it takes to disentangle oneself, having never had anything to do with land ownership [Deb had adopted a traditional academic view of the post-war world].

The real cause of all this socialistic nonsense is Cowardice – political and moral cowardice – and the system of universal suffrage will always encourage cowardice. As long as quantity instead of quality elects to rulership we shall never have honest or wise rule, and it's not a bit of use trusting to the next comers, for human nature does not change.

We at Oxford and Cambridge, are viewed with suspicion by Government and especially by Labour for the very reason that we are selective bodies and are largely independent of the yelling pack, not that any salvation will come from these places, no men could succeed where the system is wrong, but in spite of Royal Commissions they will remain selective and stand for quality and tone while the other centres solicit for the "masses".

No, I think the whole matter is entirely dissociated from Government and public and stands thus. The Senate will, under pressure, build a School of Geography, and because of its poverty it will be the minimum size and barely suitable to include the Scott Polar Research Institute. An endowment will at once relieve the Senate and ensure a proper standing as a memorial building. So much from the University point of view, from the point of view of all who can rise above the slough of politics and pettiness and see England as a long list of great men the establishment of a proper memorial to the Pole Party is a matter outside the public entirely. It is to the future men – real men, not the Daily Mail public – who still have a few ideals left or the vision to recognise past greatness.' (SPRI 559/57/10)

As far as Cherry was concerned, Deb was mainly thinking of a Scott memorial, but not yet dissociating it from a School of Geography. He forecast considerable financial problems with both the University Senate and the Government. He seems also to have changed his opinion from his views a decade earlier in the Antarctic, where he had frequently expressed his personal admiration for the crew-members of the shore party, as distinct from the gentlemen scientists and ship's officers. He considered that recruitment to these academic bodies would necessarily be a highly selective one.

Deb was not to be disappointed; the eventual establishment of the Scott Polar Research Institute attracted many young members of the Oxford and Cambridge Mountaineering and Explorers' Club – of whom Gino Watkins and John Rymill became the best known – and fulfilled Deb's expectation of 'real men'.

This seems to be the first reference made by Deb in his writings of a full title for the Institute and for a designated building for it. At that time he could not have expected that the Institute would have been founded within a few months. He wanted the endowment as 'a proper standing as a memorial building' to the polar party, and a place to engender the spirit of polar exploration.

From the letter to Cherry-Garrard (quoted in full in Chapter 4), it is clear that Deb had seen the necessity of some separation of the two academic institutions – Geography and Polar Research, the former essentially a teaching department and the latter a memorial foundation to Capt. Scott. He concluded his letter to Cherry:

'I wanted to know your opinion about the latter, that is whether you do not agree that by analogy, if by nothing else, the Pole Party has never been yet been properly appreciated, and secondly whether a private, that is a University, recognition in the form of perpetual memorial, is not the best way in which it can be done.'

This letter was penned in June 1920; by November of the same year Deb's lobbying for a memorial fund at the RGS in London, within the University Senate and amongst his influential friends, had paid off. A memorial to Scott's polar party was recognised on 26 November 1920 as the foundation of the Scott Polar Research Institute, which became the first polar institute in the world.

For Deb it was a new dawn; he was established as a lecturer in the Department of Geography, and at the same time was the principal entrepreneur for a new research institute in Cambridge University. He could hardly have expected such a novel turn of good fortune. The Board of Geographical Studies had recommended, on 24 October 1918, that a two-part Tripos examination should be established leading to honours examinations; this was approved in January 1919 (*Cambridge University Reporter*, 1918–19: 274, 432). At the end of the first year a previous, or preliminary, examination was held with Part One at the end of year two. This consisted of six papers: physical geography; political and economic geography; cartography; history of geography; anthropogeography; and regional geography. For Part Two, candidates would offer not less than two, and not more than three, selected from four papers: geodetic and trigonometrical surveying; oceanography and climatology; historical and political geography; and economic and commercial geography.

Philip Lake had been appointed the first RGS Reader in Geography in 1919, and Deb was the Society's Lecturer in cartography and surveying from the same year. The first honours degrees in Geography were awarded in June 1921: two candidates achieved first class results – J. A. Steers (who had already taken the geography diploma in 1917) and J.H. Wellington. James Alfred Steers stayed in Cambridge and was appointed an assistant lecturer in physical geography and would eventually succeed Deb as Professor of Geography in 1949. Thus the strong emphasis on the teaching of physical geography was maintained early in the Cambridge department, and strengthened further with Steers' appointment. Other appointments of demonstrators and assistant lecturers in the 1920s included R.W. Stanners (economic geography) and Mrs Margaret Anderson (biogeography), who along with Deb and others were still lecturing in the Department at the end of the Second World War.

Deb continued to work with Philip Lake until Lake's retirement in 1926. Deb then was promoted to Lake's title of Reader, and in 1931 was made Professor, the first in the subject within the University of Cambridge. The partnership of Lake and Debenham was harmonious and fruitful, as it was based on the belief that geography had at its core physical geography.

Philip Lake (1865–1949) was born at Morpeth, Northumberland. He first studied geology at the Newcastle College of Science, and matriculated at St John's College,

Cambridge in 1884. He was placed first class in both parts of the natural science Tripos, and followed this with a brief spell in the geological survey of India before returning to Cambridge. In the formative years of the Department of Geography, Lake was appointed lecturer, then reader and head of the department, posts which he held until his retirement in 1928. He was remembered by former student and colleague, Alfred Steers, 'as a teacher he was excellent. He had a quiet sense of humour and a marked ability to present his material aptly' (Steers, 1949: 115). Lake lived on in Cambridge after his retirement and was a frequent visitor to both the Geology and Geography Departments. Debenham was Lake's natural successor, with his own degree in geology from Sydney University and his field experience in Antarctica.

Throughout the 1920s and 1930s, the emphasis on physical geography as the principal foundation stone of the study of geography was kept going in Cambridge by the appointment of Steers as assistant lecturer in 1920, and later by William Vaughan Lewis, who graduated in 1929. Lewis and Steers both specialised in geomorphology (the study of the formation of physical landforms), and both gained international reputations for their work. Steers also specialised in coastal geomorphology, including the exotic study of coral reefs, and Lewis in glacial and glaciated landscapes as well as the origins of river valleys and associated forms. Lewis was appointed a university assistant lecturer in the Department in 1933, and would, but for the freezing of posts during the war, have most probably been promoted to a full lectureship by 1940. In the event he had to wait until 1945 for this advancement. Lewis tragically died in a motoring accident in de Witt, Iowa, in the United States in 1961.

In the 1920s, the Department of Geography left its temporary rooms in Downing Place at the rear of the Baptist Chapel and shared the accommodation built for the Department of Forestry. (The rooms, thus vacated, were taken over until after the war by the Faculty of Music until it, in turn, moved to new premises in West Road, Cambridge. In 2006 the space was occupied by a wing of the Department of Archaeology and Anthropology.) Deb and his colleagues continued through the 1920s and early 1930s to press the Senate for new buildings. In 1933 the Department of Forestry was moved from Cambridge to Oxford, allowing some expansion for the Department of Geography. A major building programme was then contemplated which would give the Department a home of its own. In January 1929 Deb prepared a private memorandum for the Secretary of the General Board of the University on 'The present scheme and future plans for the Geography Department'. He argued that geography had both a human and a physical side and that different schools of geography interpreted the emphasis to be laid on the subject in different ways: 'At Cambridge the emphasis is definitely laid on the scientific side because both the present and the late Heads of the Geography Department feel convinced that a great part of the "Human Geography" of other universities is purely descriptive and limited, while the scientific side of the subject is comparatively untraversed and is unlimited in its future." Deb continued to state that, as far as was known, no other university School of Geography attempted a really practical course in physical geography, and therefore the Cambridge school would be attempting something new. This was not intended to indicate that other branches of the subject, such as economic, historical and ethnographic, would be ignored. He added that the survey course was already established and deemed adequate. The new regulations would aim to turn out a new pattern of geographer, qualified as practical geographers in the sense that they would be able to undertake field and laboratory measurements under the headings of climatology, hydrology and geomorphology. The memo made clear the position from which Deb was viewing the subject, for he added, 'no graduate would be accepted for a position in a geographical expedition except one who had followed such a course as a University-trained physical geographer' (Debenham, 1929).

Deb was instrumental in designing a new department building on three floors, which incorporated the former Department of Forestry, the entire building being located along the back of the New Museums site, contiguous with a boundary with Downing College. Below ground level there was a lecture theatre to seat 150 and a commodious store to house all the survey instruments. On the first floor was built a smaller lecture room and staff offices, and above this a departmental library and map room. On the uppermost floor was planned a practical laboratory to take all the first-year students for cartographical and survey classes. Apart from the usual services there were research rooms for postgraduate students and offices for secretaries. The building had a general entrance for undergraduates and the public, where the signs of the zodiac were inscribed in the portals of the stonework, presumably a reference by Deb to his interests in navigation. There was a separate, smaller entrance for the permanent academic and support staff. A condition of the new building was that it should, at first, be shared, and the former Forestry accommodation was taken by the small Department of Geodesy and Geophysics, which held co-habitation until 1955.

Deb made space available along the corridors and around the walls of the Department of Geography for attractive maps and photographs of striking landforms and of eminent geographers and explorers. In the Library he placed antique globes and wooden copies of ancient surveying instruments. The Department was regarded with great envy by similar but less fortunate departments in other universities throughout the country. The building came into full use in 1936.

The next phase of building did not take place until the 1980s, when a fourth storey was added, the old cartographic lab remodelled and full computer facilities installed. The Cambridge Department continues to hold a premier place for teaching geography and conducting research in the subject, not just in the United Kingdom, but in the wider academic world as well.

An important legacy of Lake's tenure of his geography appointments was the publication in 1915 of *Physical Geography*, a book which rapidly became a seminal text, not only for generations of students reading the subject in Cambridge, but also for many others in the English-speaking world. The book was reprinted many times and passed through several editions well after Lake's death. The contents were divided into three parts: The Atmosphere, The Ocean and The Land. The fourth edition was published, revised, enlarged and reset, in 1958, under the editorship of Professor Steers with help from W. V. Lewis and Gordon Manley for the chapters on meteorology. Manley had graduated in Cambridge in1923, became a celebrated climatologist and meteorologist, teaching in Birmingham, Durham and Cambridge before being appointed Professor of Geography at Bedford College, London, in 1948. Manley was one of many potential lecturers in the subject, and several future professors, who ultimately gained appointments elsewhere in the country having had their first initiation into the physical basis of geography in the Cambridge lecture rooms and field excursions.

Deb also maintained his firm belief in the importance of teaching appropriate field survey techniques in order that cartographic representation should be learned. In the geography laboratory, students were required to complete cartographical exercises which included the construction of map projections for atlas maps, and to provide some knowledge of the cartographical techniques used on published maps. All first-year students were instructed in the use and care of surveying instruments in the field by afternoon sessions around Cambridge for the production of maps and plans by simple processes of chain, prismatic compass, plane-table and levelling. Deb wrote two texts specifically for these exercises (*Map Making*, 1936 and *Exercises in Cartography*, 1937).

For the most promising students, residential camps were held by Deb in parts of Yorkshire and Derbyshire, and Steers organised field mapping of such coastal features as Scolt Head Island off the north Norfolk coast (see Steers, 1966). Vaughan Lewis went occasionally further afield to examine glaciated landscapes in Iceland and parts of mountainous Norway until the Second World War prevented foreign field trips.

In 1928 the International Geographical Congress had its meeting in Cambridge, and Deb was appointed Secretary to the Executive Committee. On 9 June 1928, Deb sent Hugh Robert Mill a ticket and badge for the meeting, though expressing his disappointment that Mill was not able to address the Congress on the importance of the study of geography. He added, 'if you cannot no-one else shall'. On 27 June Deb wrote again to Mill to say he had been unwell, 'tooth trouble has spread to my ear, and I am stone deaf on the left side, and pains at the back of my neck.' He was later discovered in his rooms in the Geography Department and had to have hospital treatment for a mastoid, but wrote again to Mill on 23 July 1928 to say that he had recovered sufficiently to 'do a little work', and might contemplate a short holiday in Switzerland. His work schedule was particularly heavy at this time; he was Director of two institutes, neither of which had permanent headquarters buildings. He was engaged with the Senate of the University over a suitable site for geography, and with the RGS, several government ministries and well-wishers over a memorial building to Capt. Scott and the men who died with him. He was also having some friction with members of the Management Committee, notably James Wordie, who thought Deb should resign and a successor with polar experience be appointed. Deb consulted his trusty confidant H. R. Mill and carried on, but he continued to have periodic bouts of illness and deafness throughout the rest of his life. These were probably related initially to his war wounds in Salonika, but emphysema, brought on by his continual cigarette smoking, plagued him in later life.

On 25 January 1935 Deb wrote to tell Mill that he had been made President of the British Association Meeting for the Advancement of Science at Norwich. His presidential address would be on 'The value of polar exploration', a subject on which he had delivered a paper to the RGS as early as 20 December 1920.

Deb also taught elements of hydrology, and in 1938 had transformed the lower basement rooms of the new Institute by constructing a hydrological laboratory. It consisted of several water tanks for the creation of water processes in miniature and for their measurement. The principal of these were a stream curve, a trough for the simulation of tides, a stream flume with delta tank and a tank for producing the action of breaking waves. By a simple gearing mechanism it was possible to reproduce the movement and periodicity of tides. The laboratory could accommodate some 12 to 14 final-year students to learn techniques of research. It was possible to construct such depositional features as spits, offshore bars and submarine dunes. This innovative experimental work was possibly unique at that time amongst university geography departments.

Unfortunately in the early years of the war the apparatus had to be dismantled and placed in storage to await its return after the war was over. In 1946 the lab was reconstructed and brought back into use as an important teaching adjunct (see Debenham, 1942: 541–2). It was recalled by W. W. Williams (1901-1995), who graduated from the department in 1925 and became a professional surveyor in the Survey Department of Ceylon. He later returned to Cambridge as Lecturer in Geography in 1938, but was soon involved in the war as a Major in the Royal Engineers. He maintained that many of the preliminary calculations for the beach profiles at Anzio and Salerno in Italy and for the D-Day Crossing of the English Channel owed much to Deb's teaching and to his lab work. Bill Williams returned after the war in 1945 to continue lecturing in the Department and to act as Bursar of Fitzwilliam House.

As early as 23 July 1929, Deb wrote to H. R. Mill to say: 'Also I am thinking of a study of the Cam river system. I should like to make this part of the Field Work for the Tripos, similar to work carried out by the British Association Committee in the early part of the century on the Medway and Exe.' He asked Mill if he knew where the recording gauges had gone. Certainly during the war he led parties of undergraduates to the Fens to examine the hydrological regimes. The students referred to this work as 'going fenning'. They were instructed in the theodolite measurements of fenland posts as part of a survey which would lead after the war to the creation of a new Denver sluice, the pumping heart of Fenland. Soon after his retirement in 1950 from both the Department of Geography and the SPRI directorships, Deb was asked to examine the hydrological conditions of rivers flowing into the Bechuana swamplands of South Africa (see Debenham, 1948 *Report on the Water Resources of the Bechuanaland Protectorate*: 1–85; and *The Water Resources of Central Africa*: 222–33).

During the war years the intake of undergraduate students to read for the geographical Tripos was naturally limited by enrolment of potential candidates into the armed forces. Some students straight from school were admitted (they were either ineligible for war service or were allowed to complete their military service after graduation). The School of Geography was, however, host to the evacuated geography department of Bedford College, London, and Deb was kept very busy with large numbers of cadets from both the Air Force and Navy, who were seconded on six-month courses in navigation, and also serving members of the Royal Engineers for surveying. They were taught primarily by Deb, assisted by Mr Benest, and had lectures in the department and theodolite practice in the grounds of the University's Officer Training Corps and in the gardens of Deb's home, 23 Cranmer Road. Deb wrote a manual for the Navy and Air Force cadets, *Astrographics* (1942). This included laboratory exercises from the flat roof of the geography department. Deb reported, as ever, to Hugh Robert Mill and on 28 July 1942 he wrote, 'As a result of my book on navigation I am being sent 200 odd cadets instead of only 40, and also 120 Royal Engineers for survey work.' Some of the students seconded from the armed services were billeted in vacant college rooms.

Although the teaching staff were somewhat depleted during these years, there were sufficient numbers to maintain the courses initiated by Deb since 1920. Physical geography was continued by Deb, Steers and Vaughan Lewis, biogeography by Mrs Margaret Anderson, economic geography by Stanners and Thatcher, historical geography by Jean Mitchell of Newnham and Clifford Darby, and political geography by Harriet Wanklyn. They were assisted by recent graduates who were still around in Cambridge. By special dispensation of the University, in order to release more personnel for the war effort it was, at that time, possible to graduate in two years instead of the usual three, a practice continued after the war for those returning after military service.

By 1945 Deb was in need of a change to recuperate from his wartime workload, and had an extended leave granted so that he could carry out his work in Africa. He returned to Cambridge on his retirement in 1946. The appointment of Professor of Geography and Departmental Head was made to his long serving colleague, James Alfred Steers (1899–1987), thus maintaining the tradition of the teaching of general physical geography, particularly for the paper on physiography, a Cambridge anachronism which lasted until 1969 (see Stoddart, 1986: 211). In other geography departments the subject had been translated into the more restricted science of geomorphology, the study of landforms. In 1960 a young graduate from the Oxford

Department of Geography, Richard J. Chorley (1927–2002), was attracted to Cambridge to continue the bias towards the physical sciences. This Cambridge bias towards physical geography continues, with a particular emphasis in 2007 on glaciology, although many undergraduates take alternative options in human geography.

CHAPTER 4
A Centre for Polar Research

First thoughts about the creation of either a centre or an institute for polar research came to Frank Debenham when he was in the Antarctic climbing the slopes of Mt. Erebus in November 1912. He recalled this in his account of the formation of the Scott Polar Research Institute (SPRI, or 'the Institute'), in a paper published in *Polar Record* to celebrate the 25th anniversary of the foundation of the Institute (Debenham, 1945: 223–35). The Institute had been closed during the war, and this was the time for its re-opening to full academic work and to the general public. A celebratory dinner was given, and the Vice-Chancellor, Henry Thirkill, Master of Clare College, reiterated this Antarctic origin of the Institute:

> 'The idea was simple in form, namely, to provide some place where polar explorers might meet and learn from one another's experiences. After a period of some fourteen years, the idea was hatched in 1926, when the Institute was started in a single room in the Sedgwick Museum, in which Mr Debenham, as he then was, was working on the surveys and geological collections of Captain Scott's Last Expedition.' (*Polar Record*, 1946)

In fact, the decision to found a Cambridge institution for polar studies was actually taken some time before this date, and Debenham argued for its inception with the approval of the Senate of the University in a Grace dated 26 November 1920:

> (1) 'That the Trustees of the Captain Scott Memorial Polar Research Trust be informed that the University would welcome the establishment of the proposed Polar Research Institute at Cambridge, and concur in the suggestion that it should be associated with a building for the School of Geography.

> (2) That, subject to the approval of the Trustees, temporary accommodation be provided in the Sedgwick Museum and that the funds available for building in the meantime be allowed to accumulate.' (University Grace, 26 November 1920)

It was to take some time before the funds had accumulated sufficiently for a new single-purpose building to be contemplated, so that the Institute building was not finally opened until 1934, and by that time it had been divorced from the proposed marriage to a School of Geography. Although the latter was opened in 1936 with Frank Debenham as the first Professor of Geography, Deb maintained that November 1920 fixed the Cambridge Institute as the first such international institution in the world. However, it did in fact beat the inauguration of the Russian Arctic and Antarctic Institute of St Petersburg by only a short lead. The latter was founded only a few months later, and today employs several hundred personnel compared to the relatively smaller numbers at SPRI.

Deb had been discussing his plans whilst in the Antarctic with his climbing companions, Raymond Priestley and Charles Wright. They were concerned that the records of the *Terra Nova* Expedition, together with any equipment and survey instruments that were brought back, should have a central repository. When the Mt. Erebus group of climbers returned, in early December 1912, to their base in Shackleton's old hut at Cape Royds, Deb began to write down their ideas for a 'Polar Centre', which was later altered to a 'Polar Institute'. He had come across some blue-lined foolscap 'noble stationery' in Shackleton's cubicle, and felt it was appropriate for his commitment of these seminal first thoughts, which initially appeared as those of a dream project. Although this first stage has been repeatedly referred to, it is curious that none of it is recorded in Deb's journal of the Mt. Erebus climb written at that time (Debenham, Journal IV). Hugh Robert Mill wrote to Deb asking to see these original first draft suggestions, but Deb replied on 22 May 1947, from the Department of Geography, that:

> 'the first sketchy notes were written in Shackleton's hut, early in December 1912, after the search party had returned with news that Scott and Amundsen had both reached the Pole. It was on Shackleton's beautiful blue paper. I scribbled all over it and it may now be lost.' (SPRI, MS 100/23/1-78)

When Deb, Priestley and Wright arrived in Cambridge in 1913 the First World War was imminent, and the former Antarctic explorers volunteered for military service; the prospect of building a polar institute had to be pushed to the back of their minds. There were some attempts to pull together the scientific reports from *Terra Nova*, and Sir Arthur Shipley, Master of Christ's College, was approached and he in turn wrote to Sir Kenneth Muir Mackenzie, Chairman of the Trustees of the Captain Scott Fund:

> 'Now for the Antarctic! As I dare say you know, the majority of the scientific staff were Cambridge men, and five of these who have brought

back collections have written to say that they wish to work them out up here. I understand that Commander Evans has told them they may work out their own collections, and presume this means they may choose the place. The Professor of Zoology and the Professor of Geology have offered to put ample accommodation at their disposal, and to give laboratory attendance, re-agents, and every other facility. This will be a considerable saving.

Then I am hopeful that Caius will give one, or possibly two Studentships. Still John's also may be able to help. My College is, I fear, too poor to give Nelson any money: but they might give him a certain status and hospitality. Nelson was a student of mine.

Nothing can be done with regard to finance until the Government tell us what they feel they can do for Lady Scott and her child, Mrs. Wilson, and the other relatives of those lost their lives.

There is a big debt (how much I am not sure), but possibly somewhere in the neighbourhood of £20,000, perhaps more, and that I presume will be the second charge on the Fund. There ought to be enough left over to provide these young men with a couple of hundred and fifty a year on whilst they are working out their researches. It is difficult to say how long this will take. The collections in Zoology are very great. I am, however inclined to think that three or four years should see the end of it. There will also be the expenses of the publications. However these things gradually settle themselves.' (SPRI 1453/172)

This letter was written on 21 August 1913 from Christ's College Lodge. Before any substantive action could be taken about it the Great War had intervened, and the former Antarctic explorers were scattered to various military activities.

By the time the war had ended in 1918, James Mann Wordie was also a Cambridge resident and a frequent visitor of Deb's. Wordie (1889–1962) had been to the Antarctic, as a young geologist, with Shackleton on the ill-fated *Endurance* Expedition, and had to suffer the deprivations of a castaway on Elephant Island before the final rescue. He went to the Antarctic again with Sir Ernest Shackleton in the 1921–22 *Quest* Expedition, when the leader died in South Georgia and was buried in the cemetery at Grytviken.

Deb considered that he had several influential friends who would lend their support to his plans for a polar centre in Cambridge. Cambridge seemed always the obvious choice: Edward Adrian Wilson was a Caius man, as were Deb and Charles Wright, Edward Nelson had been at Christ's College, and Griffith Taylor had worked there before the war. Raymond Priestley was a graduate of Christ's, whilst the most significant contributor from Oxford was Cherry-Garrard. Moreover, the Mountaineering and Explorers' Club, which carried the spirit of exploration to cold regions in the 1920s and 1930s, was a joint venture between young men of the two universities. Some of the other polar enthusiasts who were consulted favoured Oxford; a few, like Bernacchi, physicist on Scott's *Discovery* Expedition, regarded London as the best location. In a short note to Deb, Mill indicated that William Speirs Bruce, the Scottish Arctic and Antarctic explorer, had established an oceanographical laboratory 'where for years he has been carrying on valuable research in Edinburgh. The new scheme must be arranged so as to avoid any injury to the prospect of his institution' (SPRI, letter from Mill, 2 February 1920, uncatalogued). This was no competitor of Deb's proposals, and Bruce's Institute, though well mounted and much visited, lasted only from 1907 to 1919.

Deb returned to his tasks in Cambridge after demobilisation in 1918. Foremost amongst them were for two permanent centres of learning: a School of Geography and a polar institute. Both, at that time, had only temporary homes. It would be another ten years before Deb was made the first Professor of Geography, although he was to become Reader in 1926 to succeed Philip Lake. He realised that the University was likely to provide funding, ultimately, for a School of Geography, as the subject had proved popular and applications were rising. On the other hand, he had many doubts about any official funding for an institute, which would be a memorial building and a research centre rather than a place for the teaching of undergraduates. He began to canvass his small circle of friends and to lobby such academic bodies as the Royal Society, the RGS, and relevant government departments like the Treasury and the Admiralty. His closest friends were Cherry-Garrard, a relatively rich young man, and Sir Hugh Robert Mill, an eminent scientist, formerly Librarian of the RGS. Both had liaisons with the corridors of power in Whitehall, and Mill had written the most influential work on Antarctic exploration published at that time, *The Siege of the South Pole* (1905).

Accordingly, Deb wrote a long letter to Cherry-Garrard on 23 July 1919, from rooms at 48 Lensfield Road, Cambridge, indicating his movement toward geography, away from geology. At this stage in his planning he considered the possibility of combining his polar centre in the same building as the Department of Geography.

'My Dear Cherry,
Sorry I have not answered your note earlier, have been rather swamped with affairs just lately as my class of surveying has swelled to 160 and demand the whole day. But I have been intending for some time to write to you on a matter, which demands a somewhat lengthy preamble and a personal one.

I think I have got my foot on the bottom rung here unless something very good offers in Australia I shall probably stay here. But it is the geography ladder not the Geology one proper. My speciality in 1910 was Petrology, but it is now far too late for me to attempt to become a specialist in the proper sense in one branch, my work has always been on the 'regional' side in Geology rather than the 'local', and as my astronomy and physics is fairly sound I see myself gradually becoming a geographer rather than a geologist, though the two are closely linked.

So much to let you understand why I am so interested in the Geographical Department here. It is just now, after the general mix up of the world war, that everybody is taking an unusual interest in geography – not the geography of small atlases and coloured maps, but the real subject including all the branches that naturally fall under the whole name, such as: Racial, Meteorology, Surveying and Geodesy, Oceanography, Physical Geography and so on.

There is bound to be a movement everywhere to try and get the whole subject brought to its proper place, and taught in a proper way. Even here they are thinking hard of the necessity for it, but are blocked by lack of funds amongst other things. Of course in America they long ago put it on a sounder footing.

Turning to another subject for the moment, the other day I was discussing with my better half how little had really been done to commemorate Scott and the Pole Party, and wondered what was being done with the sum set aside for a memorial, and what the sum was.

The brain-wave suddenly struck me that the best form of memorial would be a School of Geography and of course one idea followed another until I ended by suggesting to myself, why not in Cambridge, why not a decent building known as the Scott School of Geography, why not make it in some sort a centre for polar libraries collection etc., and so on, some of the ideas being quite impossible, but some I think pretty sound. In fact the only thing that damns the idea is the fact that I myself am likely to benefit by it since I would hope to become a lecturer in the hypothetical School, and any-one hearing that would be biased against it.

Now of course before I go any further in the matter I must make sure of my facts, i.e. that there is a memorial fund awaiting employment, who controls it etc., etc., and whether they are likely to listen to argument. And I would like you to rack your memory on these points if you would be good enough.

I can't help feeling they would agree to the general idea of a School somewhere, though they would probably ask why Cambridge rather than London or Oxford or Manchester, or Timbuctoo! The only answer to that is (*pace*-Christchurch and A.C.G.), the Expedition on the Science side was chiefly Cantabrigian, that Wilson was a Cambridge man and that it is a rising School of Geography (or will be when F.D. gets a decided footing). Incidentally that with any luck one member of the Expedition might be on the staff of the School.

Actually it would be far better if the suggestion came from some very big gun. So I want to keep myself in the dim background if there is anything in the idea likely to fructify.

My own memory on the matter leads me to think that there was a memorial fund set aside, a portion for some public statue or other and a larger portion for aid in Antarctic Exploration, but how hard and fast those labels are I do not know.

In any case I don't suppose the total amount is more than two or three thousand pounds, which is not enough in itself. But I think it might be made the nucleus of an adequate sum, for there are many people who are at present endowing schools etc. who would probably join in for a central object. As far as I can see these endowments here often depend on the wink of an eyelid so to speak, for the other day some oil companies gave £200,000 to the Chemistry Department here and would have willingly (so rumour has it) given part of it to the Geology School, if they had been able to meet the Geology Professor. Once the Scott School got a start I should just go and sit on million-aires' doorsteps till I wangled support out of them.

The thing uppermost in my mind is a really suitable memorial to Scott and the Polar Party, secondly the establishment of that memorial if possible in Cambridge, thirdly to wangle myself on to the staff; so there it all is in a nutshell.

I would very much like information you may have about that fund, and also your opinions on my little scheme. Of course, I am very small beer yet and as soon as it got going I should lump it on to some one whose name meant something. In the meantime I am lying low and seeking information.

Yours ever
Deb' (SPRI 559/57/8)

Cherry replied to Deb indicating that he had been badly hit along with other major landowners in respect of taxation and his financial position was not so good as Deb imagined. He seemed also to object to a private effort of the kind suggested by Deb, as this would be releasing the Government of its responsibilities. Deb was some-what affronted by Cherry's reaction and replied on 2 June 1920, railing against the Government, against socialistic legislation, and for no apparent reason against univer-sal suffrage:

'Consequently the alternatives are to clear out of the country and buy an island in the Pacific, or sit still and watch the ruin. But I think you are wrong in considering our project in any sense a gift to the Public or Government representing it. If the idea of a memorial were a statue in a public place – for the public to scrawl on – or a museum for kiddies to play on wet days, or something of that sort, then I would agree with you.

But when it is a project to endow a department which has nothing to do with the public, and to which the public are not admitted, the case is quite different'. (SPRI 559/57/10)

Deb hastened to reassure Cherry that the money for his scheme was not likely to be considered 'public money'.

It was clear that Deb now saw the work ahead as his true mission in life; it was to be his contribution to his former colleagues who had died amongst the snow and ice of Antarctica, and he no longer saw a Polar Institute in co-habitation with a School of Geography. The latter, important as he recognised it to be, appears to be of secondary importance. In the years ahead he would put behind him his views about 'public money'. Nor was he averse to soliciting funds from government sources.

Eventually, Deb recollected the Scott Memorial Fund that had been raised by the Lord Mayor of London. When the news came through in 1913 of the tragic deaths of the five men of the Pole Party as they were returning after reaching the South Pole, but without priority, the nation witnessed an overwhelming outpouring of grief. The national newspapers were published with black edges as though the deaths were those of members of the monarchy. The Scott tragedy was seen as an event of heroic proportions. The Lord Mayor of London called for contributions to a Fund to assist the dependants of those who had died. The response was incredible; in a short time the sum of £76,000 was raised. When the widows and relatives had been provided for, there was still a substantial sum remaining. Deb now enquired about the uses to which this remainder might be put, and he drew up a memorandum to be submitted to the Trustees of the Scott Memorial Fund. This he outlined in a long letter to Cherry, sent from his Lensfield Road address, dated 30 May 1920:

'I am enclosing a copy of the memorandum which we, i.e. Priestley, Charles Wright, myself, and Wordie (of Shackleton's last show) drew up and forwarded to the Trustees suggesting a Scott Polar Research Institute. The Trustees were the Lord Mayor, the President of the Royal Society (Thomson), and the President of the Royal Geographical Society (Younghusband). They have been entirely persuaded by it and although their decision is not to be made public until further details have been arranged they have made their decision finally.

As you will see the Institute will fulfil quite a number of needs and its activities may be condensed into the following:

1. A reference library of the ordinary type, but strictly polar.
2. A depository for original records to do with polar matters (from point of view of research this is most important).
3. A practical museum of polar gear containing either samples or descriptions of everything from rations to plans of ship.
4. A set of research rooms for use in polar research, either working out reports as we are doing, or casual inquiry such as working up a paper on say, History of N E Passage, or types and evolution of sledges etc.

It will, therefore, when reasonably well equipped, afford information and if necessary training to the following:

1. Leaders of prospective expeditions, who will find something about everything he needs for his show, besides the latest charts and descriptions of the part he hopes to visit.
2. Polar scientists, i.e. who can examine all the past reports published, also much of the original scientific rewards, also the types of instruments used in the past and the specimens.
3. Historians or general enquirers into the past events of polar travel.' (SPRI 559/57/9)

Deb envisaged a centre where those engaged in polar work might meet, foreign as well as English explorers, and where appropriate could borrow instruments from stock. He continued to Cherry: 'All that may seem too roseate a view to take of the future of the Institute', but although the matter is still *sub judice*, the few people who had been spoken to 'were tremendously enthusiastic'. H. R. Mill, for instance, had agreed Cambridge as being the best place and would help it immensely with literary donations. The American Arctic explorer Vilhjalmur Stefansson was more interested than almost anyone, and had promised all the North American polar literature he could lay his hands on. Other famous names had been canvassed, including representatives of Admiral Sir Leopold McClintock, the Markhams and Nares families (Sir George Nares was Captain of *Challenger* on the 1875–76 Arctic Expedition), and the President of the Norwegian Geological Society had written with promises. Deb added that a good deal would depend at first on the Director, or whatever title would be given, and made the surprising suggestion 'We hope that Priestley will take that on'. Certainly Priestley was backing these proposals, but it was Deb who was making all the running. Deb had a list of possible benefactors. He indicated that at that time the Trustees' plan would be for a wing for a new School of Geography, and they had allocated £6,000, leaving another £6,000 for maintenance. Deb realistically thought that it would be two years before the Institute would be properly housed, during which time there would be an accumulation of materials in the rooms being used in the Department of Geology. He maintained that the Admiralty had a lot of 'original stuff they do not know what to do with', and the RGS had a little. The rest would come from private hands where the owners had lost all interest in the possessions. Pointedly he indicated, 'I refer to journals etc., not relics. The Institute doesn't want the cap that Sir Edward Parry used, or Franklin's false teeth; the RGS is the proper place for such things!'

Deb continued to press upon Cherry the validity of the memorial nature of the building:

> 'Scott, so far, has been the only name to figure in talk of memorials, and that is not right. One cannot talk of a "Pole Party" memorial, yet in some way other names should figure. One idea was that special parts of the building should be endowed, such as the Wilson Library of Geography, the Bowers Lecture Theatre, and so on. Another idea and I think a better one as far as Bill's name is concerned is to have a Readership endowed in his name. That is all the more proper from his close connection with this University. Perhaps a Readership in Vertebrate Zoology would be the most apt under ordinary circumstances, but if our idea goes through it should certainly be the Readership in Geography, so as to keep the connection between the R. F. Scott building, and the E. A. Wilson Readership.'

Deb goes on to explain to Cherry that at Cambridge the Readership is a University appointment: 'It is held, at present, by a nice little chap called Lake, and will be held for the next twenty years by him. There is no Professor of Geography nor is there anyone here good enough for the post.' Deb obviously, in 1920, had not envisaged Lake retiring in 1926 and the readership being awarded to him; nor was he so presumptuous to consider himself for a future professorship, which was actually conferred in 1931. Deb was proposing to approach various Expedition men to help in the endowment of a building, but 'for a memorial to Bill I must admit we are thinking of you [Cherry]'. His persuasive argument continued, 'No-one was so intimate with Bill as you were, no one had a higher opinion of him; no one except Birdie went through such awful times with him. The most minor members of the Expedition would couple Bill and Cherry together in their minds.' (Deb was, of course, thinking of the awesome journey taken by Wilson, Cherry and Bowers in search of the Emperor penguin's eggs at the Cape Crozier rookery in July 1911, described in Cherry's own book *The Worst Journey in the World*.) If Cherry liked the proposal and cared to contribute, 'I can imagine nothing more pleasing to Mrs Bill, members of the Expedition, or the many profound admirers of Bill's character.'

Deb could not forecast how the general public would react to these proposals, but believed that the proposed statue in London, Waterloo Place, was not enough:

'I am sure that if, twenty years hence the readers of Scott's diary and the other versions, if any, of the party's unconquerable courage can merely point to a statue in London as a memorial they will not think highly of this generation of Scott's followers. It was the grandest end in all polar history and cannot but be a beacon to all future explorers of decent type, and to commemorate it in a more tangible way than a statue seems a small thing.

The Institute if well run will be a memorial appealing to polar people, but to the general public it will mean nothing much. If every surveyor or geographer that comes from Cambridge (there are 70 a year at present) does all his work in a building commemorating that party of five men, the world will not forget.

It must seem peculiar to people like Atch and Campbell that such a very minor member of the show should be shoving at this business, but it has got into my bones somehow. My own contribution to the funds is to be an endowment for an annual lecture on the Pole Party, or something in connection with them by the most prominent man, (of the type of Nansen, for instance), that can be obtained once a year, in the Scott Building.

As for Ponting and Evans I don't suppose they'll see anything except a fool asking for money; but over the former there is a hold of a kind. If he refuses to grant his rights (lecture and otherwise) for 3 or 4 months to us, for raising money for this, then he is a double-dyed scoundrel, and I don't think he will refuse [presumably Deb was referring to copyrights that Ponting might hold on his illustrations]. No-one in Cambridge except Shipley knows of the scheme, the present V.C. is much too busy to remember my mentioning it once to him, when he was very keen, but it has now been swamped by other matters as far as he is concerned.' (SPRI 559/57/9)

This long and important letter, closely written, to Cherry expresses more than any other communication extant Deb's passionate wishes to commemorate Scott and his colleagues, and to combine a suitable memorial with a research centre for polar studies in Cambridge.

Deb's special pleading with Cherry seems to have fallen on stony ground, as Deb received the reply again that Cherry was suffering from the deprivation of land taxes on his estate at Lamer, Hertfordshire and that there was no substantial financial contribution likely from that quarter. Nor did the suggestion of specific personal endowments in the names of Wilson and Bowers lead to positive action. The name of Scott became paramount (and when much later in 1998 an extension was added to the library, it was in the name of Ernest Shackleton rather than any member of Scott's *Terra Nova* Expedition). The recommendation of Priestley as the first Director of the Institute is an interesting one; certainly Priestley had played an important part in preparing papers and canvassing opinion, but perhaps was simply too modest to offer himself. In the event, by the time the Institute was officially inaugurated in 1926, Priestley had moved into an important administrative role as Assistant Registrar of the University, and later in a distinguished career he became for many years Vice-Chancellor of the University of Birmingham. Frank Debenham, who had done so much to create the Institute, was the obvious choice for the first Director.

The memorandum composed for the Trustees of the Lord Mayor's Fund was sent via Sir Arthur Shipley, delivered in November 1919, to Sir William Soulsby, the Honorary Secretary of the Captain Scott Memorial Mansion House Fund, but was not discussed by the Trustees until their next meeting in March 1920. It had been decided by the Trustees that the £76,000 Fund should be divided as follows:

- a half to the widows and relatives of those who were lost
- about £17,000 set aside for publications of the scientific results
- £12,000 for a memorial statue to be erected in Plymouth
- a sum of £10,000 set aside as a 'Polar Research Fund'.

This allocation had been minuted by the Committee: 'to be devoted to an endowment fund in aid of future polar research, the income to be applied either annually for the encouragement of such work as may arise, or allowed to accumulate until such an occasion should present itself.' This was the apportionment that Deb was seeking.

In the memorandum sent via Shipley to the Scott Trustees, Deb rehearsed the points he made in his letter to Cherry. He maintained that all polar expeditions were very expensive, and that the interest on monies invested from the Fund would never be likely to make a major contribution to an expedition. Far better to give the money set aside for polar research to a centre in Britain where scientific records could be kept, equipment stored and aspiring explorers could make their plans. Such a centre should be located in an established academic atmosphere, preferably in a university. The Royal Geographical Society was such a centre, but only in a general sense; they had no laboratories, no research rooms, their library could not specialise purely in polar information, and moreover their contact with all the necessary scientific personnel could not be guaranteed. The memorandum argues that polar research is not purely geographical, it concerns itself with problems of biology, geology, geophysics, meteorology and many other allied sciences. Although London, with its many learned societies, might appear to be a proper place, it should be remembered that polar research is done by comparatively young men, not normally yet in touch with such ancient societies, and men who require laboratory facilities such as the societies seldom possess. These requirements are best met by a university.

The memorandum then aimed to persuade the Trustees that the University of Cambridge was pre-eminent in these respects. Of the four most prominent South Polar expeditions of English origin since the beginning of the century, 16 young men were from English universities, of which 13 were Cambridge men, two from Oxford and one from Manchester. As far as could be ascertained, no other English university than Cambridge had provided facilities for this work. On general grounds, so claimed the authors of the memorandum, the polar centre should be a part of a Department of Geography. It was believed that the authorities of Cambridge University proposed to erect a special building for the School of Geography, which might be enlarged appropriately to house a wing for polar research.

Although Deb and Priestley still considered the matter essentially *sub judice,* it was vital that others within their polar circle of close friends should be aware of proceedings. Deb had received permission to go ahead: Lady Scott had expressed her support in a letter addressed to H.R. Mill, and favourable opinions had been received from Evans, Cherry-Garrard, Campbell, Wright and Atkinson. Deb had also discussed his proposals with Mrs Wilson (Bill's widow) and Mrs Reggie Smith (Scott's publisher friend). James Wordie and Ernest Shackleton were also privy to these strategies.

On 29 March 1920 Deb heard, via Shipley, that the Trustees were impressed by the application, and on 5 May 1920 Deb was summoned to a meeting at the Mansion House, where the Lord Mayor, supported by Sir J.J. Thomson (Cambridge University) and Sir Francis Younghusband (RGS) questioned him in detail about the proposals. The outcome was favourable, and the following day a letter was sent from the Trustees to the Vice-Chancellor of Cambridge stating that the Trustees were 'prepared to grant £6,000 toward the provision of a suitable Wing, or Annexe, forming part of a larger building devoted to Geography'. The long summer vacation intervened before all the constituent bodies of the University could consider the offer, but on 2 November 1920 the Council of the Senate issued in the *University Reporter* its agreement to the proposals from the Lord Mayor's Fund, that temporary accommodation should be provided in the Sedgwick Museum, and that the funds available should be allowed to accumulate. Thus, following Deb's thoughtful preparations and well-laid plans, the University of Cambridge reached a decision and proclaimed a Grace on 26 November 1920 which truly launched the Scott Polar Research Institute.

Deb could now make public this decision, and on 20 December 1920 he delivered a lecture to the RGS on 'The Future of Polar Exploration', which was printed in the *Geographical Journal* for March 1921. Deb spoke ostensibly about the history and the future of polar expeditions to both the Arctic and Antarctic regions, but his principal objective was to reveal his notable coup on securing for Cambridge a new centre for polar research. The President of the RGS, at the conclusion of the lecture, commented:

'Our scientific men are not always as guileless as they appear on the outside. You will observe that all that the lecturer has been saying, first of all in his artless way about oceanography, geology, and meteorology was leading up to the point that a Polar Research Institute should be established, and then that the one place in the whole world in which one should be founded was at the Cambridge University. By an extraordinary coincidence the lecturer is a member of the University of Cambridge, where he holds the Lectureship in Surveying and Cartography which bears the Society's name.'

Sir Ernest Shackleton and Edward Atkinson then gave the venture their blessing. The President, very charitably, concluded by saying, 'I did put in a humble plea for the Royal Geographical Society, but I could not prevail against the eloquence of Mr. Debenham on behalf of Cambridge' (Debenham, 1921: 182–204).

By careful stratagems, fine eloquence and a good cause to argue, which resonated readily with the Trustees of the Fund, the first hurdle had been overcome. Deb felt very happy with the result and returned to his temporary home in the Sedgwick Museum of Geology. Here he finished his '*Terra Nova* Reports on Maps and Charts', and started to prepare his collections of polar artefacts. Expenses were mainly covered by gifts from private sources, but the Trustees gave £350 for furniture, some books and charts. Soon visitors began to arrive, and Deb was delighted that young men from Oxford and Cambridge sought his help in planning expeditions, principally to the Arctic. Foremost of these was George Binney (later Sir George) from Oxford, and James Wordie (later Sir James) from St John's College, Cambridge. Binney made a reconnaissance of the Svalbard archipelago, making use of a seaplane, and Wordie explored parts of Greenland in 1923, 1926, 1929 and again in 1934, and had landed on the remote island of Jan Mayen in the Norwegian Sea and completed the first ascent of its highest mountain there, Mount Beerenberg.

However, the condition made by the Trustees that the new Polar Institute should form a special wing of a new Department of Geography proved more of a structural handicap than an economy. The University seemed to be dragging its feet and no plans were immediately forthcoming for a new Geography building. Accordingly, Deb renewed his petitioning to the Trustees of the Lord Mayor's Fund. Deb asked in a letter to Sir William Soulsby, dated 10 February 1925, that the promised £6,000 should now be made over to the University, allowing one-quarter to be used as capital for maintenance. In a letter of 23 February it was agreed finally to hand over the £6,000 and to consider the use of the remaining £7,000. This was more than Deb had contemplated, nor had he asked for it. On 12 March, Sir William sent a letter to Deb from Sir Charles Sherrington, President of the Royal Society, acceding to the request that the Fund should now be extinguished and the whole balance transferred to Cambridge. On 9 May 1925, the Vice-Chancellor (Professor A.C.

Seward) replied: 'The University of Cambridge gratefully accepted the generous offer of the Trustees of the Scott Memorial Fund to present to the University a sum of money for the erection, endowment and maintenance of a Captain Scott Polar Research Institute.' The proposal for a polar centre was no longer tied to the collateral condition of a building for Geography. The Trustees made some advisory conditions: 'that the memorial character of the building should be kept in mind and suggest that £6,000 be set aside for the building and upkeep.' They desired that its erection should not be deferred for a longer period than ten years. Deb had fought his battle and won, for these were precisely the conditions he had advocated in his earlier memorandum to the Trustees. In fact, the construction of the Scott Polar Research Institute was completed in 1934, two years before the erection of a new building for Geography.

The Senate confirmed Deb as Director of the Institute, and a Management Committee was appointed which met for the first time on 27 January 1926. The Vice-Chancellor, Professor Seward, was made Chairman and he served for ten years until he left Cambridge; the RGS appointed Dr H.R. Mill as its representative and he served until the outbreak of the Second World War. The other three members were Raymond Priestley, James Wordie and Deb himself, who acted as secretary to the Committee, but without voting rights. All three members continued in office until after the war.

Lensfield House, the first home of SPRI (SPRI)

To celebrate the inauguration of the Institute a ceremony was held in the after-noon of 22 May 1926, followed by a dinner in Downing College. The opening address was to have been given by the distinguished Norwegian Arctic explorer, Fridtjof Nansen, but he was prevented from attending by the coal strike of that year. The dinner was a fitting tribute to polar exploration; the guests included nine of Scott's men and five from Shackleton's expeditions. Admiral Sir George Egerton of the 1875 Expedition was the oldest member present, and Deb was particularly delighted to see there his former Professor from Sydney, Sir T.W. Edgeworth David, who had been on the *Nimrod* Expedition of 1907–1909. Lady Scott (later Lady Kennet) was present with her husband, Commander Hilton Young (later Lord Kennet). Messages of congratulations were received from the high and mighty of polar exploration: from Baron de Gerlache of Belgium, Dr Charles Rabot and Dr Jean Baptiste Charcot of France, Dr Erich von Drygalski of Germany, Dr Otto Nordenskjold of Sweden, and Dr Knud Rasmussen of Greenland.

The Institute could not have had a more propitious start. In 1927 a move was made from the attic rooms of the Sedgwick building to an old house, recently bought by the University from Sir George Stokes, the original owner. This was Lensfield House at the corner of Lensfield Road and Panton Street; until 1929, the new Institute had to share the premises with the School of Architecture. The house was quite commodious, with fine lawns for the restoration of kayaks and sledging equip-ment and for the giving of small receptions. One of the earliest was in 1928 for members of the International Geographical Congress attending the Cambridge meeting in that year.

Deb soon realised that it was impossible to organise the Institute single-handed, and many volunteers were forthcoming on an occasional basis. More significant was the help provided by Miss W.M. Drake, who came to offer her services in 1927. She was a teacher of chemistry at the Girls County School, which shared premises in those days in Collier Road, off Mill Road. Miss Drake was living then at 43 Maid's Causeway in Cambridge, and was relatively close to both her teaching duties and to the Institute. She spent most evenings between 5.00 and 7.00 p.m. and at weekends dealing with administrative duties, labelling museum objects, preparing pictures for exhibition and so on. Mrs Oriana Wilson had presented a magnificent collection of Edward Adrian Wilson's watercolours to the Institute. Miss Drake carried out all these duties without any permanent payment until the last year in 1930–31, when the Management Committee regarded her position as official by making her Assistant to the Director at a nominal salary of £50 per year. Miss Drake was known to her friends as Winifred, but from the start Deb nicknamed her' Francis', and as 'Francis Drake' she remained, even to the signature she penned on Deb's letters. This famil-iarity became, to the uninitiated, a matter of some confusion. Not only was this a confusion of gender, but some writers wondered if this was the same Francis Drake who had been with the *Terra Nova* ship party as secretary to the expedition.

General plan of Lensfield Road site, 1926 (*University Reporter*)

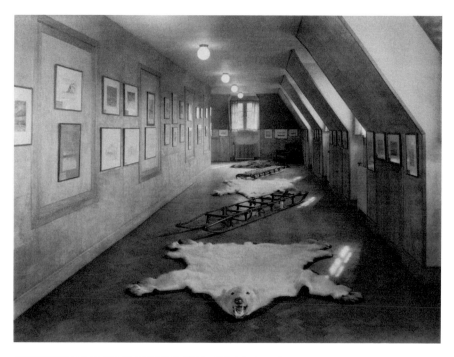

The original Wilson gallery of
watercolours (SPRI)

Miss Drake was the first of a succession of 'Deb's girls' who held the position of Assistant to the Director until Deb retired in 1946. They all worked tirelessly doing any job that came to hand, acting as Deb's secretary, museum curator, hostess to visitors to the Institute, or more humbly, in emergency, scrubbing the floors. Several left the Institute only to marry eligible young men who left for careers in Africa. 'Francis Drake' (later Mrs Gordon Hayes) was replaced in 1931 by Betty Creswick (Mrs James Moore), a former student of Deb's, and she in turn left to be married in 1938 and moved to live in Sudan in 1942. From 1938 Dorothy Featherstonehaugh (Mrs John Wright) filled the post, followed by Mrs Benest, the wife of one of Deb's surveying colleagues, assisted by Harriet Wanklyn (Mrs J.A. Steers), until 1945, and finally, from 1945 until 1953, the post was occupied by another of Deb's geography students, Elizabeth Rought (later Mrs John Peake). They carried out their duties in a spirit of friendliness and thoroughness, attending to the niceties of entertaining as well as the routine business. Miss Drake began an album, 'Hints to Future Assistants', which contained such advice as the kind of jam preferred by Dr Mill and how many lumps of sugar he would like. A helpful atmosphere of friendliness prevailed; no legitimate enquirer was turned away, even schoolboys writing about a polar explorer were sent the information they sought.

Deb published an article in the *Geographical Journal* for July 1926 rehearsing the aims and conditions for the new Captain Scott Polar Research Institute. He explained

Deb reading a book in the Museum (SPRI)

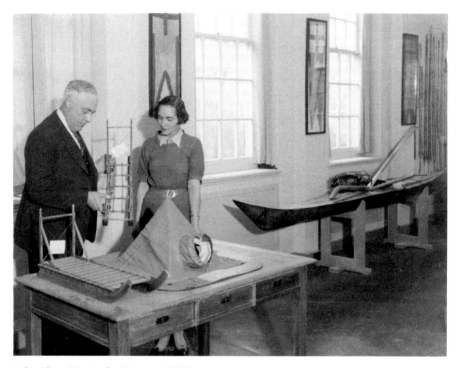

Deb with a visitor in the Museum (SPRI)

that the balance of the Mansion House Fund, £12,000, had now been transferred to Cambridge: £6,000 for the foundation and £6,000 for maintenance. He was now seeking the rest to ensure the completion of the Institute, another £8–10,000. He repeated his hopes that a building of some elegance, consonant with its memorial function, should be designed, which would include a Map Room, Library, Museum, Picture Gallery, storage facilities and rooms to carry out polar research. At that moment they possessed some 300 books on polar matters, instruments and polar gear, photographs and watercolours, including a large number of negatives and 130 enlarged prints given by Herbert Ponting. Although these collections were, at that time, in the attic rooms of the Sedgwick Museum, Deb invited anyone interested to visit at any time.

In 1928, Deb was feeling the strain of directing a Department of Geography, and at the same time he was nurturing the infant Polar Institute as well as acting as Secretary to the International Geographical Union Meeting in Cambridge. He had suffered a short spell in hospital for a mastoid to be removed. Deb wrote to Mill indicating that at the next meeting of the Management Committee the discussion would be about a successor to himself as Director. He suggested Wordie, 'who is well off and therefore not a strain on the Institute's finances'; Wordie had suggested Priestley, but he was also overburdened with work as Assistant Registrar to the University. Deb explained to Mill that he thought the Director should have a nominal salary, and an Assistant should act as Secretary. Miss Drake had done all the routine work in her spare time, and without pay, and Deb had no salary but only took £50 towards expenses.

On 24 February 1929, Deb sent Mill an estimate of his breakdown of the costs of a new Institute:

a.	Building with furniture	£10,000
b.	Maintenance, rates, fuel, light	£ 2,000
	(£100 per annum, capitalised)	
c.	Permanent officer	£ 5,000
d.	General maintenance	£ 6,000 (i.e., the existing fund)
	Total	£23,000

At that time the funds, transferred from the Lord Mayor's account, stood at £7,000 for buildings and £6,000 for maintenance, totalling £13,000. George Seaver, a friend of Wilson's and an important polar biographer, had suggested applying to the Carnegie Fund of America for financial help. Deb would discuss the matters with Mill at the latter's next visit to Cambridge. In the meantime, Miss Drake had indicated that she would reluctantly welcome an honorarium, as her salary as a school teacher was only £220 per annum. By 1931 Deb had been in touch with Sir Edward and Lady Hilton Young (Lady Scott), who had agreed to approach the Pilgrim Trust of America for a grant, made up as: £5,000 to complete the building fund, £3,000 for the maintenance fund, and £5,000 for the salary of a Director and his Assistant. The outcome was a grant of £4,000 for the buildings account.

At last things were moving, but Deb was, understandably, impatient. He wrote to Mill on 9 July 1931:

'The process of getting our building is gradually taking shape in the leisurely manner beloved of Universities. The Council of the Senate has appointed a Syndicate to deal with the matter, the Grace being as follows: "That the Vice-Chancellor, Professor Seward, Sc.D., Master of Downing College, T. Knox-Shaw, M.A., of Sidney Sussex College, Treasurer, Professor Debenham, C. F. Cooper, M.A., of Trinity Hall, Sir E. Hilton Young, M.A., of Trinity College, J. M. Wordie, M.A., of St John's College, and R. E. Priestley, M.A., of Clare College be appointed a Syndicate to prepare a scheme for the erection of a building for the Scott Polar Research Institute".'

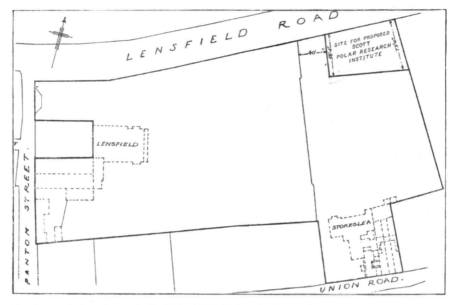

Development plan of new site for SPRI, 1932 (*University Reporter*)

Deb apologised to Mill for the latter's absence from membership of the sub-committee of the Syndicate, the only member of the Management Committee to be so treated, but this was explained by a regulation of the University that only members of the University could sit on a syndicate of this kind (SPRI 100/23/13).

He proposed, nonetheless, to keep Mill informed and ask for his advice by proxy. Deb was forecasting 'some fireworks' at the next meeting of the Management Committee, for he and Priestley believed that two members of the Syndicate might try to block recommendations from the Syndicate. Wordie had already said that the money raised so far would be better spent on a polar expedition.

However, by 1932, the site for the building on Lensfield Road had been confirmed by the University and an architect, Sir Herbert Baker, appointed. Deb could hardly have hoped for anyone better, as Sir Herbert was the University's Professor of Architecture. This was all reported to Mill in a letter, dated July 16 1932. Deb described the first sketches:

> 'Baker has a more or less rectangular building with the entrance on to Lensfield Road. The front door leads into a hall divided into two halves by dome-like ceilings on which he is anxious to put the routes of explorers in golden lines. I am much more anxious to have the Polar Regions on the floor of the hall, and there is no reason why both should

Deb's birthplace, The Vicarage, Bowral, NSW Australia (Debenham family)

Sedgwick Building, the attic room, the first polar collection (P. Speak)

First Geography Department rooms, Downing Place, 1920s (Shirley Wittering)

New Geography Department, Downing Site, 1939 (Shirley Wittering)

SPRI frontage on opening in 1934 (SPRI)

Plaque of Gino Watkins (SPRI)

Lady Scott's statue *The Offering* in front of SPRI (C. Swithinbank)

The Library, c.1980
(P. Speak)

The new
Shackleton
Memorial Library
rotunda (P. Speak)

not happen, that is to say, something picturesque on the inside of the domes, and a reasonably accurate map in 'material' on the floor below them.'

Deb was worried, however, because Baker had warned that if he gave the Syndicate all requisite floor space for the museum, library and gallery, the cost would be at least £1,000 more than they had. The Syndicate had increased the money allowable to £8,250, but this was likely to be insufficient if Deb was to marry his concept of a memorial building within one large enough to function as a polar research institute. Deb went, once more, holding out his begging bowl for grant money from American philanthropists. He also persuaded Mill to write a letter to *The Times* stating the case that the building they wished to erect should not be spoiled for 'a happor'th of tar'. Some additional monies were essential. There was little success for some time, but Deb persisted with the plea 'do not let us build to a minimum'; he wanted a fine building of a particular quality. In a letter sent by Sir Herbert Baker to H.C. Marshall at University offices, St Andrew's Street, with a copy to Deb, the architect attempted a compromise: he had reduced the area very slightly and agreed an estimate with the quantity surveyor of £8,250, allowing for good yellow brick with a limited amount of stone dressings, and for a cornice and balustrade probably in artificial stone. It includes deal painted joinery, except for the front door, and pine block floors generally; heating by radiators, and the installation of electric light without special fittings. In order that the Committee could examine the alternatives he included the following estimate:

Extra for facing the whole building in Weldon Stone £1,500
Ditto Ketton Stone £1,800
Cost of portico exclusive of statue or carving Weldon Stone £825
Ditto Ketton Stone £900 (SPRI 100/23/19)

Sir Herbert's design was for a more-or-less rectangular building in neo-Georgian style with the interior showing an influence of Lutyens. It presented an elegant frontage to Lensfield Road, with a central entrance surmounted by a bust of Capt. Scott. Deb must have had some success with his fundraising, for the finished building had oak block flooring throughout, with oak panelling and book cases in the Library. The decoration of the interior domes in the vestibule caused much argument. Deb preferred decorative designs on each dome representing Arctic and Antarctic exploration, with maps of each region formed in a mosaic composition floor. This was changed to the painting of the maps on the domes with representations of important expedition ships and names of explorers. Arthur Hinks had written to Seward on 21 November 1934 about the names to be painted on the maps. He asserted that it was irregular in a memorial building to use names of living explorers, but reminded the Committee that Gino Watkins and the Greenlander, Knut Rasmussen, should be included if the Norwegian, Hjalmar Riiser Larsen, and the Russian, Boris Vil'kitskiy were to be there. Deb wrote back to Hinks, sending a copy to H.R. Mill, explaining the rationale for the inclusion of some names and the exclusion of others. The Management Committee had agreed that Wordie and Deb would have the choice of placing the ships and names on the maps. How could anyone choose the priority of naming and the selection of expeditions? What showed initiative and was heroic for one person could have been repetitive and simply fortuitously successful to another. It was therefore decided that the underlying principle should be a commemoration of those men who were responsible for the discoveries that were on the map. This indicated that the discovery of hitherto unknown lands should be the chief guide in selection, and that each name should be placed approximately opposite the sector of the discovery. In practice this principle worked quite well, although some parts of the Polar regions had been given more attention than others, and so the competition for placement was strong and some names had to be omitted. Somehow Ross (Sir James Clark) had been omitted in the final list; fortunately, this was noticed in time to be added to this pantheon of explorers. The only names which appear both in the North and the South were Ross and Amundsen, and the only ships common to both Poles were *Erebus* and *Terror*. The *Fram*, Amundsen's ship, was condemned to omission from the South, as she did not attempt ship-exploration when transporting Amundsen to

Informal group in the Old Library, 1964, including, *from left*, Terence Armstrong, 3rd, Harry King, 5th, and from right, Gordon Robin, 6th, and David Drewry, 4th (SPRI)

the Bay of Whales, though critics might have considered this decision based on the patriotism of the selectors! Deb pointed out that the list could not be comprehensive if artistic considerations were considered (SPRI 100/23/38).

The work was commissioned from the artist Macdonald Gill, assisted by Priscilla Johnston. Deb and Wordie had the task of climbing the gantry, lying on their backs, like Michelangelo painting the roof of the Sistine Chapel, in order to select the correct placing of the ships and the explorers' names. Hinks was invited to a Management Meeting on 7 February 1935, where Wordie and Seward managed to placate Hinks, 'the only critic of the names on the domes', and Deb won the day by insisting the illustrations should not represent a roll of honour, rather a coronet of names of those explorers responsible for the discoveries in each map sector. If change was proposed and came to more than £50, then Deb would immediately resign! Fortunately all was happily resolved.

The remaining external decoration to be settled was the inscription to be carved in the upper stonework of the balustrade. In a letter Deb received from Baker dated 6 May 1933, an amended inscription was sent for approval: *Quaesivit Arcana Poli, Videt Dei*. It had been suggested by Dr H.A.L. Fisher (Master of Wadham College, Oxford) to Lady Young, and was checked by a classical scholar of the University. A free translation is: *'He sought the secrets of the Pole, but he sees the secret of God'*.

The floor of the vestibule of the museum was changed from Deb's suggested maps of the Arctic and Antarctic to images of the nine stars of the Great Bear, *Arctus Major*, on one side, and the four stars of the Southern Cross, *Crux Australis* on the other. The capitals of the pillars supporting the domes had carvings of polar bears for the Arctic and penguins for the Antarctic. Internal classical pillars in the Library were of carved oak, and the panelling and shelves of the same wood. On the keystones outside above the two large windows were carved, by Charles Wheeler, A.R.A., symbolic representations of a polar bear, and an Emperor penguin feeding its chick. In the early years of the 1930s, the prices of building materials and the cost of labour were considerably lower than in later years, so the Institute could be built economically compared to prices in the years to follow. The final cost included an upper storey to be used as an art gallery, the walls of which were lined with thick African plywood. Deb did not have to scrimp and save, as he had feared, and the architect managed to produce one of the most elegant buildings in Cambridge. The builders were the local firm of William Sindall, Cambridge. The *University Reporter* of 1 December 1926 listed the original account of £12,000 as 'paid for Lensfield'; in the accounts issued on 8 November 1934 the following sums were given:

Paid, Sir Herbert Baker	£214 18s 8d
Sindall, Contractor	£5,000
Decorative Painting	£118

And on 14 November 1934 further sums are noted:

> Paid, Sir Herbert Baker   £85 6s 10d
> Sindall, Contractor   £1,537 2s 2d

In addition to carving the bust of her husband Captain Scott for insertion in an alcove above the main door, Lady Scott presented the Institute with a fine bronze statue of a nude, a young man with arms outstretched and face turned to the heavens. It was erected in the small garden at the front of the building. The bronze had been modelled by the young Kathleen Bruce (1878–1947, later Lady Scott), and she had taken as her subject an undergraduate, A. William Lawrence from Jesus College, whose brother later became the celebrated 'Lawrence of Arabia'. The young model was later appointed as Cambridge University's Professor of Classical Archaeology, and in the 1940s the Director of the Botanic Garden. In the pedestal the inscription reads: *Lux perpetua luceat eis* (May eternal light shine upon them). An account of the work of Kathleen Bruce as a sculptress can be found in *Self Portrait of an Artist* (Kennet, 1949), where the bronze is illustrated and called 'The Offering'. Others have given it the title *'Spirit of Youth'*.

When the building opened it was separated from the road by iron railings. Deb was concerned that the bronze might provoke passers-by to some defacement, or undergraduates to some mischief. Accordingly, he planted a hedge outside the Institute, which eventually grew high enough to hide those parts of the statue that might cause embarrassment. Successive Assistants to the Director, and later also the Museum curator, have had the job of cleaning the statue periodically!

The site on which the Institute stands became the first University building on this southern side of Lensfield Road, which before the nineteenth century was known as Cross Road. Land became available only after the passing of the Enclosure Act of the Eastern or Barnwell Fields, Cambridge in 1807. It made land available for urban expansion to the south of the city, and from about 1830 the built-up area known as New Town was created from that part of the former Common Fields described as Ford Field, and outlined by Trumpington Street, Lensfield Road, Hills Road and the northern limit of the Botanic Garden (from 1835), some 80 acres in total (see Bryan and Wise, 2005). In 1811 an Act was passed allowing the sale of these common fields for domestic residential building, and lands were allotted to both private and corporate bodies; these included the colleges, Addenbrooke's Hospital, and others who were then free to sell to private developers. Until the nineteenth century, university and college buildings were confined to the historic medieval centre around St Mary's Church and along the Backs. By the middle of the nineteenth century, expansion was taking place in the new Museums site south of Downing Street, and included the new Downing College and such important buildings as the Sedgwick, Anthropology and Archaeology Museums, together with many Science Department buildings. This

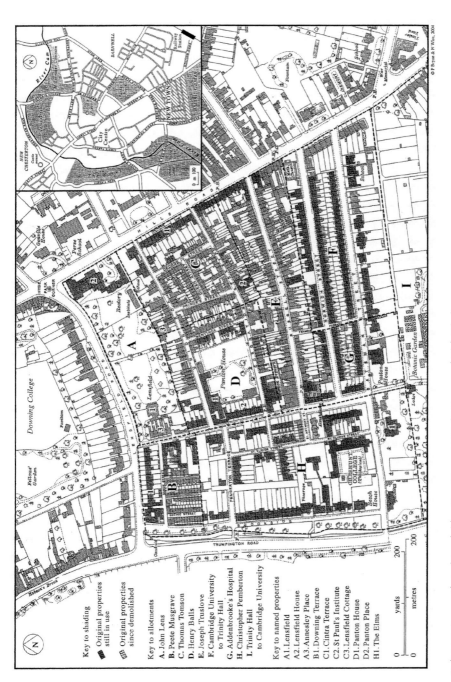

Key to shading
- ▨ Original properties still in use
- ▨ Original properties since demolished

Key to allotments
- **A.** John Lens
- **B.** Peete Musgrave
- **C.** Thomas Tomson
- **D.** Henry Balls
- **E.** Joseph Truslove
- **F.** Cambridge University to Trinity Hall
- **G.** Addenbrooke's Hospital
- **H.** Christopher Pemberton
- **I.** Trinity Hall to Cambridge University

Key to named properties
- A1. Lensfield
- A2. Lensfield House
- A3. Annesley Place
- B1. Downing Terrace
- C1. Cintra Terrace
- C2. St Paul's Institute
- C3. Lensfield Cottage
- D1. Panton House
- D2. Panton Place
- H1. The Elms

Ordnance Survey Plan of Cambridge New Town, 1927 (P. Bryan and Nick Wise) development stopped at the north side of Lensfield Road. Whilst the central part of New Town was built over with a mixture of villas and terraced houses, the northernmost part, i.e. that fronting on to Lensfield Road and bounded by Panton Street, Union Road and Hills Road, was owned by John Lens, a former member of Downing College who lived and practised law in London. He was associated with William Wilkins, a local architect who was responsible for much of the new Downing College (1807–1873) and whom he employed to build a house for his own use, around 1811, close to the junction of Panton Street and Lensfield Road. He called this house 'Lensfield'. He had built another larger residence in 1810, naming it (somewhat confusingly) 'Lensfield House', for local banker Lulian Skrine. This house was demolished in the mid-1880s to allow for the building of the Catholic church, from Hyde Park Corner along Hills. Almost inevitably, the road was given its present name, Lensfield Road. There were fine gardens around both houses, and Lensfield eventually came into the ownership of the University and was offered to Deb as temporary accommodation in 1926. The plot of land adjacent to the Catholic church was made available, by the University, for the Institute in 1929. At that time it had a good-sized garden at its back leading to a small exit to Union Road. The next phase of development was a major one, the designation of the rest of John Lens' field for the Chemistry Department, which was started in 1953. Although the Institute managed to keep land for building at the rear, its former gardens have been lost, and Deb's apprehension of a giant Chemistry neighbour has now dominated Lens' old site. 'Lensfield' was demolished, and Chemistry, one of the largest Departments of the University, built to a strictly utilitarian, modernist style, has like a behemoth continued to grow until the present day and now overshadows the Scott Polar Research Institute.

Deb and his Assistant, Betty Creswick, began to move into the new Institute in July 1934, taking the collection of polar artefacts and the Wilson pictures, though the design of furniture was still with the architects.

The official opening took place on 16 November 1934 by the Prime Minister and Chancellor of the University, Stanley Baldwin, accompanied by college dignitaries and several guests from overseas (*Polar Record*, 1935: 2–9). A celebratory lunch was first given in the Hall of Gonville and Caius College, attended by, amongst others, Sir Edward and Lady Hilton Young (Lady Scott), Sir George Egerton of the 1875 *Nares* Expedition, Capt. Mikkelson from Norway, and Dr Lauge Koch from Denmark. The party moved after lunch to the Senate House where Chancellor Baldwin gave a fulsome speech in praise of exploration, with particular reference to British explorers in the polar regions:

'This building provides a library for those who are led, as men are today, to this work. Those who are going into the partly known and the little unknown, they may study there what has been done, how difficulties

Antarctic Dome, interior of the Museum (SPRI)

have been overcome, what equipment is necessary, what equipment has been proved to be superfluous or bad, and they may have all the knowledge that has been gleaned and left for them by those who have blazed the trail. And, similarly when they come back they can there, make their records, and leave behind them whatever they have to leave for the benefit of those who follow in their footsteps.' (*Polar Record*, 1935: 2–9)

The party then proceeded to inspect the Institute, followed by taking tea in the Hall of Downing College. For Deb, who had waited 14 years for this occasion, it was a time of great elation and satisfaction to see his longed-for dream come true. It was a truly bi-polar institute, covering the polar regions of both hemispheres, unlike many of its successors elsewhere in the world devoted either to the Arctic or to the Antarctic.

In the next few years Deb continued to add to the Museum's exhibits and to purchase or invite as a temporary loan pictures, sculptures and other works of art to adorn the walls and the interior. It became a centre of fine art, open to the public, as well as a centre for polar research. On 24 November, Deb wrote to tell Mill that they had received some 60 or 70 visitors a day in the past week, many leaving donations, some as much as £5, and one of £10, for the purchase of books. The domes had still to be painted, but this would be done the following year. Otherwise it was complete.

Francis Drake (Winifred) left the Institute in 1931 to marry Gordon Hayes and to emigrate with him to a tea plantation in Nyasaland, but before she left she had discussed with Deb the desirability of publishing a biannual journal, *The Polar Record;* it would give the Institute credibility as an academic centre of research, and promote its image. The first issue was published in January 1931 by Cambridge University Press, price one shilling. Deb was the general editor, but he relied, as usual, on the advice of H.R. Mill to vet the copy. The *Record* set a standard which has been maintained ever since, not an overt scientific periodical, but a journal in which the general reader would find polar articles of interest. Issue 1 comprised: a summary of the aims of the *Polar Record;* obituaries of the Norwegian polar explorers Fridtjof Nansen and Otto Sverdrup, Captain William Colbeck (of *Morning,* the vessel that went to the relief of *Discovery,* Scott's first Antarctic expedition), and Lieut. Charles Royds (who had served with Scott on *Discovery); accounts of the British Arctic Air Route Expedition, 1930 and the Antarctic Expedition, 1930–31; a proposal from meteorologist George Simpson; an account by Bernacchi of the British Polar Exhibition held at Central Hall, Westminster in July 1930 (Bernacchi had given £200 of the profit to SPRI); a review by Wordie of *Andree's Letters;* and a list of books on polar matters in 1930.

In the 1920s and 1930s Deb was pleased to see the Institute used by young mountaineers and explorers seeking adventure in the polar regions. Chief of these were Gino Watkins and John Rymill. Watkins came from an upper-middle class family, had failed to be accepted at Eton, his first choice, and was at school at Lancing in Sussex before coming up to Trinity College in 1925 to read for an ordinary degree in engineering. Henry George Watkins (known always as Gino, an Italian diminutive, named after his grandmother Watkins) came to Deb's attention in 1929 when he became the leader of the British Arctic Air Route Expedition, seeking to pioneer air routes across the Greenland ice cap and to monitor meteorological conditions. It was seen as a preliminary to accomplishing the North-west Passage by air, so that planes could travel from Britain to the Pacific coast of North America by the shortest route, that is, flying along Great Circles drawn on air navigation charts. One of the least known parts of Greenland was the coast south of Angmagssalik and the south-eastern interior. Gino Watkins and his young companions seemed to Deb to resurrect the spirit of adventure and youthful heroism that he had witnessed on the *Terra Nova* Expedition. Most remembered of the group were Watkins, Augustine Courtauld (meteorologist), Alfred Stephenson (surveyor), assisted by John Rymill, Jimmie Scott (dog driver), F. Spencer Chapman (ornithologist), Quintin Riley (meteorologist), and Lawrence Wager (geologist, and soon to be included in a party for the assault on Mount Everest). The group left England in July 1930 in Shackleton's old ship, *Quest,* taking with them not only the traditional sledges, dogs and kayaks, but also two motor boats and two De Havilland light aircraft for purposes of surveying. One feat of great fortitude and endurance reminiscent to Deb of the Antarctic journeys of Scott and Wilson was the continual occupation of the meteorological station in the heart of the ice cap. Too far away to be regularly supplied from the coast, Courtauld volunteered to man the station single-handedly from 6 December 1930 to 5 May 1931. When relieved, he was found to be virtually completely snowed in, though in good health after his solitary watch. During this expedition Watkins became particularly adept at paddling the single Eskimo kayak.

Watkins returned to this area of Greenland in 1932 with just three companions, John Rymill, Spencer Chapman and Quintin Riley. They left Copenhagen in the supply boat *Gertrud Rask* on 14 July. At 8.00 p.m. on 20 August, Gino left in his kayak to hunt seals in Lake Fjord, but tragically was lost, presumably drowned. The others found his water-filled kayak at 3.00 p.m. with his paddle nearby, close to a glacier snout. He had shown great skill in kayaking and his distraught companions searched throughout the fjord and on land nearby, but to no avail. He was aged 25, and was considered already an explorer of first rank. In the next issue of *Polar Record* (January 1933: 5), the frontispiece carried a pencil drawing of Gino and an *in memoriam* poem by Betty Creswick:

> Regretting you, because your years were splendid
> Beyond a brilliance we shall ever know,
> We, whom your fineness stirred, who saw you go
> Smiling, as one who by the gods stood friended.

Deb and Mill requested the Management Committee for sanction to open a fund in Watkins' memory. A plaque was commissioned to be wall-mounted in the Museum, and the remainder of the funds devoted to funding polar expeditions by young explorers. By July 1933 there was a sufficient sum for an income of £50 per annum. Today (2006), this fund still exists and in 2005 awarded grants totalling £11,600 for various expeditions to both the Arctic and the Antarctic; it is regularly petitioned by groups seeking some polar patronage. The plaque of Watkins now hangs on the wall at the end of the Arctic Gallery. Gino's kayak was presented to the Royal Geographical Society to be hung in their museum in Kensington Gore, London.

John Rymill had known of Gino's wish to explore a route across the Antarctic continent, though they both regarded it virtually impossible in 1931, a time of acute economic depression, to raise sufficient funding. Rymill returned to Britain from Greenland in 1932 in order to organise an expedition to Antarctica, and was advised by Deb and James Wordie to attempt something less ambitious, a detailed topographic survey of Graham Land. In 1934, Rymill was promised £1,000 by the RGS, and given a grant from the Colonial Office of £10,000 as this land was part of the Falkland Islands Dependencies. These grants encouraged Rymill to start making his preparations for the British Graham Land Expedition (1934–37), a three-year stay in Western Antarctica. It was hoped to raise at least £15,000 without too much difficulty, and in fact the final cost was just short of £20,000. Rymill purchased an old French schooner for £3,000 and had it refitted and re-named *Penola,* after his home in South Australia. He enrolled Quintin Riley, Alfred Stephenson and Surgeon-Lieut. Bingham from Watkins' Greenland expeditions. Other members of the scientific team included the Rev. W.L.S. Fleming, geologist, Colin Bertram, biologist, and Brian Roberts, ornithologist, all of whom would later play significant roles at SPRI (Fleming and Bertram as Directors, and Roberts as Deputy Director). Other crew members were seconded from the Royal Navy, and in Port Stanley, Falkland Islands, Duncan Carse was transferred from *Discovery II* (he became much better known, on returning to England, for playing the title role of *Dick Barton, Special Agent,* in the long-running radio serial). Using dog sledging and aerial surveying the expedition demonstrated that Graham Land was part of the Antarctic continent and not, as previously thought, an archipelago.

Rymill's expedition observed a group of islands in the north-east of Marguerite Bay (on the west side of Graham Peninsula), and named these collectively the Debenham Islands, and individually by the name of each of Deb's six children: Barbara, Barry, Audrey, Brian, June and Ann. They were seen from the air by the expedition on 27 February, and surveyed from the ground in March–May 1936 (BAS Report, 1991).

Brian Birley Roberts (1912–78), a member of Rymill's British Graham Land Expedition, ultimately became one of a small band of research workers at SPRI and was held in respect – and in some fear – by junior members of the Institute. He had the most unorthodox first acquaintance with the Institute in 1929. In that year he was a pupil at Uppingham School, and came to Cambridge to visit SPRI (at that time in Lensfield House). Finding the building closed at the weekend, he climbed through an open window and inspected the Museum, left a thank-you note, and returned to school. In November 1930 he wrote to Deb to say that he was hoping to come to Cambridge as an undergraduate the following October, and asked Deb for an interview. He added that his chief interest was in natural history, and that he wished to join an expedition. Deb saw him, and Roberts duly entered Emmanuel College to read geography in his first year, and then archaeology and anthropology. He graduated in 1934. Brian led two expeditions to the Arctic: to Vatnajokull in Iceland in 1932, and to Scoresbysund and East Greenland in 1933. Brian's specialised knowledge was in ornithology, but he had a zeal for everything polar. He came to know Wordie very well in Cambridge and found a great rapport with him. Wordie saw Brian Roberts as a suitable Assistant to the Director of SPRI when Deb retired, but Deb would never agree as he found Brian impossible to work with. Deb wrote to Mill on 7 February 1945 to say that Wordie was suggesting all the wrong things for the future of the Institute. Wordie had recommended a saving on redecoration and a reduction of the length of *Polar Record*. Deb would have none of it:

> 'He has developed the sort of implacable attitude that the pre-war system of running the Institute and, possibly my directorship is ruining the Institute – only Brian Roberts can save it.
>
> 'In my view our two best publicity agents are the *Record* and the attraction of the building and furnishings, and I deplore having to cut down on both. I am very much in favour of having a man with polar experience there as Curator or Deputy Assistant the moment we can afford one, but to do it at the expense of the *Record* and the building seems to me to be very dangerous.'
>
> 'Deb indicated that he would be happy with any of the other candidates he had in mind, namely Colin Bertram, Quintin Riley and Alfred Stephenson. He added:
>
> 'On the question of the Directorship, I am rather adamant, I think a younger and less busy Director would be a very good thing, and I should like it to be a Gino Watkins man, and six months ago, I was considering seriously how and when to resign. But the re-orientation of policy as outlined by Wordie and Roberts has thoroughly frightened me for it would tend to change the Institute from a club for encouragement and information to beginners, into a formal office where questions put by the Governments would be dealt with according to civil service methods. These are the extremes of course, but under Roberts the extreme civil service aspect would predominate.' (SPRI 100/23/72)

In 1939 at the outbreak of the Second World War, Deb considered closing the Institute and making arrangements for the security of its contents. However, on 19 June 1939 Deb wrote to Robert Neal Rudmose Brown, long-serving Professor of Geography at Sheffield, to say that he had dined with the Vice-Chancellor and met Admiral Godfrey, Director of Naval Intelligence, who was asking about the setting-up of an information bureau, similar to that which had operated during the First World War. SPRI was considered suitable and Deb asked Brown, who had recently been elected to the Board of Management, if he would consider vetting appropriate names for the Bureau (SPRI 356/53/1–2). By early 1941, Treasury approval had been gained for two centres, one in Oxford and the other in Cambridge.

The SPRI building, which had been closed to the public, virtually became a Department of the Admiralty, leaving only two ground-floor rooms for the Director and his Assistant. The principal task of the Bureau was to produce Admiralty Geographical Handbooks (N1D5) for use in the various theatres of war. Wordie acted as part-time Director for some of the time, and H.C. Darby as Editor-in-Chief. Senior members of Geography and allied departments worked there on a part-time basis; at Cambridge there were 30 academics, including Brian Roberts of the Graham Land Expedition, supported by 60 experts and many others. In all, 58 volumes were produced: 28 from Oxford and 30 from Cambridge, plus an unpublished manuscript on Spitsbergen (mainly by Rudmose Brown), and notes for a volume on Afghanistan (see Balchin, 1987: 159–80). This meant that no other persons could use the building, including the Library. It was not until the summer of 1945 that the Institute was re-opened for general use, though Deb, assisted by Mrs Benest and Harriet Wanklyn, had kept routine matters in hand.

When Mrs Benest left her post in 1945, Deb informed Mill that he was considering as a replacement former geography graduate Elizabeth Rought. She had been at school at Sherborne and came up to Newnham during the war to read for the geographical Tripos. Deb had a very favourable impression of her. Elizabeth had been working in the American Intelligence Office in London, and Deb had made an agreement with her superior to release her for the Cambridge appointment. Wordie was predictable in opposing this appointment in Committee, suggesting a deferment until a man would be free to apply for the job, and was expecting Brian Roberts to be appointed. Deb's proposals prevailed. He wrote to Mill in January 1945 to say that he had approached Elizabeth by letter:

> 'saying that the work was pretty exacting, that she would have a hard job to keep herself on £4 a week after the war, and was she still of the same mind. Her answer makes me quite sure she is of the same kind as Betty and Dorothy, to the effect that hard work and short commons were a fair price to pay for the privilege of working for, and with, live people who

were mad enough to go exploring which meant hard work and short commons.' (SPRI MS Mill, 100/23/71)

In August 1944 Deb had outlined to Elizabeth the nature of this work:

'It will involve rather hard work too, as we – the selected unfortunate and I – have got to get the Institute going again. Better than ever before, we've got to wheedle this and compromise on that, stall this member of the Cttee. and encourage that, and all the time get the *Polar Record* back to its former full issue and the building to its former pleasant and invit-ing appearance and atmosphere – particularly atmosphere. The Institute is open to the public – not to children – 10–4 daily, Sats. 10–1, and the Assistant's hours are variable, sometimes just those, or longer depending on what's a-doing. Secretarial jobs are dealing with correspondence, average of 3 or 4 letters a day, at first through me, later largely on her own responsibility, keeping the small accounts etc. Sub-editorial duties are overseeing preparations of the *Record* MSS every six months, proof reading and correspondence in connection with it. Librarian duties are cataloguing and general supervision – Library is not open to public except on request to me or Assistant Director.'

All this for £4 per week; Deb knew that the appointee must be dedicated! But that was not all:

'Hostess duties are more varied, from occasional glance in the museum to explaining things to any-one interesting or interested, to answering questions and having special people to tea. It becomes a kind of club in the late afternoon, when there are polar people about, behaviour ranging from the utmost decorum with the older visitors, to debate and cushion assaults with the younger.'

In October 1944 Deb wrote to Elizabeth again:

'There's only one hurdle to be surmounted, which, as it has nothing to do personally with you, I can tell you. It is that my Chairman Wordie of St. John's, wants a certain man to take D's place, not a girl at all. He never said so to me, I only heard it today and he isn't back from his holiday yet. I think I told you before that he would probably have a duke's daughter in his pocket for the job – well, she had changed to a certain man, but the reasons are much the same.

I am fairly confident of his being sensible and giving up his plot gracefully, because I'm certainly not going to fall in with it. Anyhow the Director cannot have his plans altered by the annually elected chairman of his Ctee. of Management. Sooner or later you'd have heard that Wordie is not a very helpful chairman, but I didn't want to worry you at this stage with skeletons in the cupboard. At least there's only one skeleton, or dual one, Wordie and Brian Roberts, who are both great plotters.'

Deb complained about the last issue of *Polar Record*:

'As soon as I opened it, I got a shock, because I've been "done in the eye" again by Brian Roberts. He does the list of "Recent Polar Literature" and every time I've had arguments for him to reduce it and be strictly polar. I saw the proof for all the rest but Mrs. Ben [Mrs. Benest] said Brian had asked to correct the proofs [of *Recent Polar Literature*] and he sent it straight back to the Press instead of to me, which he should have done. Technically its my fault as Editor but I never dreamed he would run amok like this – the list is as you'll see 11 pages, nearly one quarter of the whole issue, and strays miles outside the Polar Regions.'

On 16 January 1945, Deb wrote to tell Elizabeth that he had had a word with Wordie:

'I spoke straight about Brian Roberts and he now knows that I won't have him as any kind of Assistant, and he accepts that. Incidentally I fancy he knows why too, because he himself has had a certain amount of trouble and debate with him.'

However, he did have some regard for Wordie: 'In point of fact, re Wordie, for instance, his only fault is ambition, no finer feelings, a parsimonious outlook and so on. But lots of good points as well.'

Deb does appear to have reached a fair analysis of Wordie's personality. Although unknown to Deb, but now revealed retrospectively from Mill's papers given to the SPRI Archives, Wordie sent a long telegram to Mill dated 17 June 1945 in which he expressed his doubts about Deb's fitness to carry on as Director: 'Deb is physically unfit and mentally tired and no longer himself'. He also advanced the claim of Brian Roberts for the post, pointing out that Roberts was a younger man, and had edited and written parts of *Polar Record* for some time and had good ideas about the research that the Institute should be following.

By this time Mill was himself quite ill, and had not been a member of the

Management Committee for some time; in fact, he had resigned at the beginning of the war. He appears to have ignored Wordie's advice. It was true that Deb had been unwell, but this was caused by emphysema, and he was considering his doctor's advice to take extended sick leave. In addition, he had been feeling the strains of his long-term directorships of both the Department of Geography and the Institute. In April 1945 sought medical advice and by 20 April he was writing to Elizabeth Rought saying:

'That cold of mine with shortness of breath is turning out less innocent and temporary than I had hoped. I went to the doctor yesterday and after a lot of going over and a general strafing for doing too many things he gave me the impression that I am lucky if he will let me carry on this term; it depends on X-rays and other evidence. In the meantime I am to keep as quiet as ten mice. It's all rather in the air, the only very clear pronouncement he made was that I must certainly take a year away from the Department, as soon as possible. So there seems to be a nice tangle ahead – the Dept. more understaffed than ever, and the P.R.I. more or less minus a director just when new policies are being settled. All very annoying – just the opposite of what I had hoped. Still, we won't be down hearted about it.' (Elizabeth Rought, personal communication)

In October 1945 when Deb was making preparations to travel to Central Africa for his hydrological surveys and for his recuperation, he wrote to Elizabeth again saying: 'You know Elizabeth I really ought to resign the Directorship when I return, but I don't know how I can bear it, its become a part of me, a sort of obsession.'

During this time the Institute's affairs were cared for by Launcelot Fleming as Deputy Director. In July 1946, towards the end of his sick leave and shortly before returning to Cambridge, Deb submitted his resignation operative on 1 October 1946. The Management Committee upgraded Launcelot Fleming to the post of Director.

Launcelot was Dean and Chaplain of Trinity Hall; he was a mountaineer and geologist, had been with the Cambridge Expedition to Iceland in 1932, with the Oxford Expedition to Spitsbergen in 1933, and on the Graham Land Expedition in Western Antarctica in 1934–37. He had all the credentials for the job, and in Deb's eyes he must have been 'a Gino man'. He had also served on the Management Committee of SPRI.

A luncheon was given on 22 March 1947 in Trinity Hall to mark the official re-opening of the Scott Polar Research Institute, and the Vice-Chancellor, H. Thirkill, Master of Clare College, welcomed the guests, who included Peter Scott, though his mother Lady Kennet was unable to attend. The Vice-Chancellor gave special thanks to the work of Frank Debenham, and stressed the importance in which the

University held the Institute. Similar remarks of approbation were made by the RGS and the Hydrographer of the Navy. The following Institute staff were present: Director Launcelot Fleming, Research Fellow Dr Brian Roberts, Research Fellow in Russian Studies T.E. Armstrong, Temporary Research Fellow in Scandinavian Studies J.G. Elbo, Librarian Miss D.M. Johnson, and Assistant to the Director Elizabeth Rought.

The Institute had taken an important turn away from a concentration on polar exploration and expeditions. Terence Armstrong was a Cambridge graduate, fluent in Russian, who was later to create a focus on ethnographic studies of the North, particularly the Russian North. He had served in the Intelligence Corps and had an exceptional record in important battles in North Africa and Western Europe, parachuting into the Rhineland, and was one of the first of British forces relieving the city of Oslo. Doris Johnson was the first full-time Librarian. She was well known for keeping her little pug dog on her library table! John Elbo pursued his research in Scandinavian studies. He worked for a short time in Spitsbergen, but sadly died in 1954.

Elizabeth Rought continued, at a modest salary, until 1953. At that time she had the difficult task of dealing with Brian Roberts, whom Harriet Wanklyn described as 'a large teddy bear with glasses'. However, as he was seldom there during office hours, it was easy for Elizabeth to maintain the open door of Deb's philosophy. Brian had volunteered for the Navy in 1939, but was turned down due to his short-sightedness and so worked with Colin Bertram in 1940 producing a handbook for military personnel on clothing and equipment in cold regions. In 1941 he joined the ad hoc group of advisors at the Naval Intelligence Division, based in SPRI, and was involved in the planning of the covert *Operation Tabarin*, which prepared a polar party to operate in the South Atlantic and Antarctic during the remainder of the war. Its intention was to monitor German activity in this far-distant but highly specialised theatre of the Second World War. *Tabarin* was the name of a Parisian nightclub and adopted as the code name of this expedition force. After the war ended, the organisation of *Tabarin* was used to found FIDS, the *Falklands Islands Dependencies Survey*, which in turn was transmuted into the present British Antarctic Survey (BAS). Brian was appointed to the Foreign Office Research Department on 5 February 1944, and eventually to the Polar Desk in the Foreign and Commonwealth Office.

At the Foreign Office Brian Roberts is remembered for his great efforts towards the ratification on of the Antarctic Treaty in 1959. Brian worked ceaselessly at countless international meetings and, particularly, behind the scenes in the political corridors of negotiation to create the Antarctic Treaty System (which has stood the test of almost 50 years of international scientific collaboration, almost unique in the world). John Heap, who joined Brian at the Foreign Office in 1964, said that the Treaty owed more to Brian than to anyone else (John Heap, personal communication). Brian was a prolific contributor to many polar journals: to *Polar Record* and the *Journal of Glaciology*, both published from SPRI; to official Foreign Office reports; to ornithological literature and so on. He is best remembered at SPRI for his monumental editing and annotation of *Edward Wilson's Birds of Antarctica* (1967) and for his contribution to the *Illustrated Glossary of Snow and Ice* (1966) with T.E. Armstrong and C.W.M. Swithinbank, which has become a definitive work.

Throughout his period at the Foreign Office, Brian Roberts was part-time, working from Tuesday to Friday in London and then travelling back by car to Cambridge to resume his duties at SPRI. Here he worked from Friday evening to Monday evening, through the weekend, often staying late or carrying work back home, a short distance away, to 61 Causewayside Flats in Newnham. He retired from this post only at the end of 1975, when he was replaced by Dr John Arnfield Heap. Brian insisted on seeing all the mail to check it for style and content, and would have been quite delighted if the Institute closed its doors to the general public and turned away all casual enquirers.

All who knew him recognised that he was a prodigious worker and meticulous in everything he did to the point of extreme pedantry. His greatest contribution at SPRI was his introduction of the Universal Decimal Classification system for the cataloguing of all the Library's titles.

In the early 1950s, Doris Johnson was replaced by Margaret Butterworth, who in turn was replaced in January 1955 by Harry King as Librarian and Ann Savours as Archivist and Assistant Librarian. They learned to manage the Library quite adequately during Brian's absence during the week, but their work was scrutinised by Brian between Friday and Monday on his return from London. In the Festschrift for Brian (King and Savours, 1995: 111): 'Brian set a standard of excellence, with great attention to detail, in his own work and in the work of the staff who edited *Polar Record*, catalogued the collections, and provided the bibliography at the end of the three-yearly journal entitled *Recent Polar Literature*.'

Launcelot Fleming, who had fulfilled the role of Director since Deb's retirement, left Cambridge in 1949 to take up the position of Bishop of Portsmouth and was succeeded by Dr Colin Bertram, who had recently returned from the Pribilof Islands.

In 1956 Colin Bertram retired as Director, and after a brief interregnum was replaced on a full-time basis by Gordon de Quetteville Robin, an Australian by birth, who had trained as a physicist and served at the Falkland Islands Dependencies Survey (FIDS) base in the South Orkneys at Signy. Gordon later joined the Norwegian–British–Swedish expedition of 1949–52 to Dronning Maud Land to examine the thicknesses of the Antarctic ice sheet. He returned to lecture at Birmingham University before taking up his position at SPRI in 1958. During his long service for the Institute he laid great emphasis on its scientific work, rather than on the history of exploration. Together with Stan Evans of the Department of Engineering, he developed the technique of radio-echo sounding of the Antarctic ice sheet by aerial survey. This innovation revolutionised the mapping of Antarctica's subglacial topography; much of the fieldwork was carried out by a series of annual visits by a research student of Robin's, David Drewry. The compilations were made back at SPRI, and ultimately an impressive ice atlas of Antarctica was published (Drewry, 1983).

Deb had encouraged the study of polar glaciers and was gratified by the selection of the International Glaciological Society (IGS) to make its administrative home in the Institute. The long-serving (1953–93) Secretary General was Hilda Richardson, a former Geography student of Deb's. The IGS continues to share SPRI's premises as well as using other offices nearby. The scientific nature of so much of SPRI'S present research was also recognised by its selection as the Secretariat for the Scientific Committee on Antarctic Research (SCAR), an institution which was created concurrently with the International Geophysical Year (IGY) 1957–58 by the International Council of Scientific Unions (ICSU).

Deb would have been pleased to see SPRI become a Mecca for polar enthusiasts from all parts of the world. Some come for a courtesy call, but many for a research period of weeks or months. They are attracted by the unrivalled collection of books, original expedition journals and pamphlets held in the Library. A frequent visitor in the 1990s was the Russian geologist Andrea Kapitza, from the Institute in St Petersburg and the son of the famous nuclear physicist Peter Kapitza. He came to analyse, with Gordon Robin, the remarkable sub-glacial Lake Vostok, found beneath the most isolated ice cap Russian Antarctic station, Vostok. Long series of ice coring had revealed a large lake, at depth, within the ice sheet. This collaboration led to a paper in *Nature* (Kapitsa et al., 1996: 684–6), and also to the discovery of similar sub-glacial lakes elsewhere within the Antarctic ice cap.

Under Gordon's influence a Sea-Ice Research Unit was established, led principally by David Drewry, who followed Gordon as the next Director of the Institute in 1984, and by Peter Wadhams, who was Director from 1987 to 1992. Thus the theatre of operations spread to the examination of the nature and distribution of sea-ice in both hemispheres, an important element in the contemporary examination of global warming. David moved on to become Director of BAS for a while, and then successively Head of the National Environmental Research Council (NERC), Director of the British Council, and currently Vice-Chancellor of the University of Hull. Peter Wadhams was elected to an *ad hominem* professorship in the University of Cambridge, and moved with his sea-ice unit to the Department of Applied Mathematics and Theoretical Physics.

When in 1962 FIDS was renamed British Antarctic Survey (BAS), the control was at that time invested in the Natural Environmental Research Council. It made sense, then, to gather together the scattered units. One of the units (Meteorology) was based in Cambridge, and in 1976 a new, purpose-built research establishment was opened along the Madingley Road in the western suburban fringe of Cambridge by Prince Philip, Chancellor of the University. The laboratories and offices were housed in a remarkable building, made principally of concrete with vertical ribbing to resemble a tabular iceberg when viewed from the road. After the Falklands War of 1981–82, the building was substantially enlarged to reflect the increasing scientific and political importance of Antarctica. The BAS building has never been part of the University of Cambridge and remains financed by grants from the Treasury, via NERC, but who can tell that, without the prior establishment of SPRI, BAS might well have been located elsewhere? Today it employs over 400 personnel, whereas SPRI survives with a full-time staff of some 20 individuals, but with many part-time employees and associates.

Other institutions that have recognised the academic nucleus of Cambridge as a centre for polar research, including the Cambridge Arctic Shelf Project (CASP) and the International Whaling Commission (IWC). CASP was founded by Brian Harland, senior geologist in the Department of Geology and expert on the geology of the Svalbard archipelago. After a spell in the Department, the group is now located on the Huntingdon Road. IWC seems to have been located, almost by chance, in a small house in Histon, north of Cambridge, mainly because the first and long-serving Secretary had his home there. Additionally, BAS has in Cambridge its substantial Sea Mammal Research Department at Madingley Road.

In addition to these research projects in the physical sciences, SPRI continues its tradition in the humanities. This has been due largely to the major influence of Dr Terence Armstrong (1920–96) who came as a research student in Russian Studies in 1947 and stayed at SPRI for all his professional life, retiring only in 1983. His work concentrated initially on the Soviet North, about which he wrote a seminal book, *The Northern Sea Route* (SPRI, 1952), but he researched the whole of the Circumpolar North, producing an important book on the subject, along with Graham Rowley and George Rogers (1978). Together with numerous research students, from the late 1950s and 1960s, he extended the Institute's interests in cross-cultural and multi-cultural studies of a linguistic, anthropological and ethnographic nature amongst the indigenous Eskimos, Inuit and Sami (Lappish) peoples as well as those inhabiting northern Siberia. He worked for 25 years, from 1960, as joint-editor of the Hakluyt Society's historical publications. His legacy lives on with the research of his direct successor, Piers Vitebsky, in studies of Siberian reindeer herding, and Michael Bravo's work amongst the Inuit of northern Canada. Deb would have felt proud of these developments, many of which must surpass any ambition that he had for the Institute back in 1920.

Gordon Robin, soon after his appointment, realised that the original Institute was inadequate for all its post-war requirements and ambitions. He planned for an extension which would house a new lecture theatre, new research rooms, new laboratories, new map room, and a substantial new area for the Library and Archives. The *University Reporter* issued a statement about the Institute's proposed extension on 14 June 1965, indicating that the Vice-Chancellor had managed to obtain a substantial loan from the Ford Foundation of America, in the summer of 1963, for £100,000, and Messrs

Hughes and Bicknell had been appointed architects. The plans were to increase available space for the Library of 933 sq ft [2,650 sq m] and to build a basement for a workshop, cold rooms and storage room beneath the 100-seat lecture theatre. The general contractors were the firm of Rattee and Kett, specialists in the construction of university buildings. In order to accommodate the new buildings to the old site, and to the pressures of the new Chemistry building alongside, the entrance was turned around to face the east end of Chemistry, the original entrance was closed and blocked from inside, and a new glass-fronted reception area created which formed a link between the old and the new. The original total floor area was 179 sq ft [510 sq m] and the new one 919 sq ft [2,610 sq m], thus enlarging the building five-fold. The extension was conceived as a rectangular four-storey block, built of Stamford bricks as closely resembling the originals as possible. Attention was given to important details such as the granite stone floor of reception which allowed the Arctic section of the museum to extend from its original location and therefore giving more room for the Antarctic exhibits. The floors above ground level continued the oak blocks of Deb's design, and the furniture was of oak construction. The entrance glass doors were skilfully engraved with the physical structures of snow and ice crystals. Building work began in July 1966, and the new part was occupied in 1968; alas, Deb died in November 1965 and was not able to see these new extensions. They were opened, appropriately, by an American, Larry Gould, President of the Scientific Committee of Antarctic Research, on 27 July 1968.

CHAPTER 5

Deb's Legacy to Cambridge

Frank Debenham contributed immeasurably to Cambridge academia. For 30 years, from 1919 to 1949, he lectured, gave supervisions, and controlled the progress of the University Department of Geography, first as Lecturer, then as Reader, and finally as the first Professor. For 27 of those years he was also the Director and the prime inspiration of the Scott Polar Research Institute. During the same period he sat on innumerable University and College councils and committees, lectured widely outside the University, notably to the RGS, and produced many textbooks, scientific reports and other materials on geography and on polar research. His last article was on the headless fish he discovered on the ice shelf of McMurdo Sound, published in the *Journal of Glaciology* in October 1965. Deb died on 23 November that year.

Many have wondered why he was never offered a knighthood for his contribution to British education. His close friends from the *Terra Nova* Expedition, Raymond Priestley and his brother-in-law Charles Wright, were both knighted – Priestley in 1949 and Wright in 1946. Priestley had served as Vice-Chancellor of Birmingham University for many years and also fulfilled the same position at the University of Melbourne. Wright had become the first Chief of the Royal Navy Scientific Service in 1946. In addition to these celebrated former polar explorers, Deb's polar academic colleague in Cambridge, James Wordie – who had been on Shackleton's famous abortive *Endurance* Expedition and suffered the privations of being marooned on Elephant Island, South Shetlands and subsequently joined the *Quest*, the ship on which Shackleton was to die in the Southern Ocean – had received a knighthood in 1957 'for services to Britain's polar activities'. Deb must have surely thought he was in the running for something similar.

John Heap, Director of SPRI 1992–98, in the week before he died, confessed that there had been many who had approached him, when he was still at the Foreign Office, to intervene on Deb's behalf. John added that, whilst he did not have the kind of influence that many believed, he would have been pleased to see Deb also given the noble accolade. 'Deb was essentially a people's person,' maintained John, 'and did not deliberately cultivate the loftier levels that a prospective knighthood required' (John Heap, personal communication).

Deb had received an OBE in 1919, consequent on his war service, and received many honours for his scholarly contributions. In 1948 he received the Victoria Medal of the Royal Geographical Society, of which he was Vice-President in 1951–53, the David Livingstone Medal of the American Geographical Society in 1948, and honorary degrees from the universities of Sydney (1959), Western Australia (1937) and Durham (1952). His greatest satisfaction was to see the continuing admission of young men and women as undergraduates in the Department of Geography and the international fame gained in polar research for the Scott Polar Research Institute.

When Deb retired in 1946 a presentation was proposed to him and subscriptions were invited by the new Director, Launcelot Fleming, to whom cheques were to be sent at Trinity Hall. It was suggested that the sum of £1 would be appropriate, but more could be given if desired. The other signatories to the letter for contributions were George Binney, August Courtauld, A.R. (Sandy) Glen, Lady Scott and Raymond Priestley. A presentation of a handsome cheque was made to Deb on 22 March 1947, at a party held to mark the re-opening of the Institute after the war.

The front of SPRI carries, quite properly, above the former entrance, the bust of Capt. Scott, as polar explorer. When the extension of the building was completed there were many who felt that a memorial plaque to Deb should be mounted near the new entrance. This was eventually agreed in February 1982. A discussion was held between Barbara Debenham, June Debenham Back and Philip Back, all members of Deb's family, and Terence Armstrong, Harry King and Clive Holland from the Institute's staff, together with the Chairman of the Friends, Sir Vivian Fuchs. It was agreed to ask the sculptor David Holgate to undertake the work of preparing a 21-in plaque of riven Kirkstone green slate from the Lake District, and of carving a good likeness to the family's satisfaction. This would be surrounded by a suitable inscription:

Frank Debenham O.B.E., 1883–1965
Founder and First Director, 1920–1946

The Friends provided £300 towards the cost, the rest (about £450) being met from Deb's family and other well-wishers. The result is a youthful-looking portrait of Deb, mounted on the wall by the new main entrance. It was unveiled on 14 July 1984 by a well-chosen group: Sir Vivian Fuchs, Alfred Stephenson and Mrs Frances Hayes, who as 'Francis Drake' had been the first Assistant to the Director.

When the University in 1920 agreed on the foundation of a polar institute in Cambridge it was envisaged that this would be a memorial building, but with research functions and facilities. This excluded the teaching of undergraduates and a formal teaching programme, or Tripos. Although this made it unusual in Cambridge depart-ments, it was not unique. Most Cambridge departments enrolled undergraduates for a three-year course, followed by a smaller body of postgraduate students proceeding towards the higher degrees of Master of Philosophy and Doctor of Philosophy. The emphasis on postgraduate research has been maintained throughout the life of the Institute, but has had, as its consequence, major financial and administrative difficulties. With no undergraduate teaching, a considerable income is denied to the institute; moreover, the fees charged by the University to postgraduate students are inevitably greater than for undergraduates, and consequently the demand for places smaller.

The Treasury made a direct annual grant after the last war, in recognition of the valuable information services provided by SPRI and its role during the war when it housed the naval branch of Intelligence, and other bodies continued – like the RGS, the Hydrographic Service and British Petroleum – to make some funds available. Any further expansion of a building programme would require major philanthropy. Without further accommodation for research, the possibilities for any enlargement of the student intake was minimal.

In 1980 a report of the General Board of the University recognised that the position, which had been created in 1957, of the Institute as a sub-department of Geography was somewhat anomalous, and recommended that henceforth it should become an independent department within the Faculty of Geography and Geology, and that the Advisory Committee, appointed in 1956 to replace the former Management Committee, should be continued (*University Reporter*, 6 February 1980). The General Board recognised that polar studies was not to be found as a coherent course in any other Tripos, and recommended that some teaching of the subject should be contemplated within other disciplines.

The Board had commented favourably on the introduction, in 1975, of a one-year Postgraduate Diploma in Polar Studies, and noted that it attracted mainly mature students, particularly those from overseas with experience of living in polar regions. In 1981 the Diploma was upgraded to an M.Phil. degree, which consisted of daily seminars given by polar experts from within the Institute, supplemented by colleagues from the British Antarctic Survey, the Foreign Office Polar Desk, and commercial companies involved in the Far North and South. The administration was, at first, in the hands of the Director and Assistant Director (Gordon Robin and Terence Armstrong), and later controlled by senior members of SPRI. The curriculum was essentially eclectic, but specialisation occurred in the selection of a 20,000-word dissertation as part of the examination. In 1992, with the resignation of Peter Wadhams as Director, the General Board again reviewed the Institute's financial and academic position, and recommended a reversion to the role of SPRI as a sub-department of Geography.

John Heap, who had at that time recently retired from the Polar Desk at the Foreign Office, was appointed a five-year contract to the Directorship, at the end of which the directorship was to become a part-time appointment for a member of the Department of Geography. In fact, John Heap continued, and held an executive directorship from 1997 to 1998, and Professor Keith Richards, a fluvial geomorphologist from the Department of Geography, took over from him until 2002 when the post was offered to Professor Julian Dowdeswell. Julian had been an undergraduate member of the Department of Geography, and followed this by postgraduate studies in glaciology at SPRI for his Ph.D. degree. He was subsequently offered professorships at Aberystwyth University, and later at Bristol University, before returning to Cambridge as Professor of Geography, and Fellow of Jesus College, to continue his research amongst the ice of both the Arctic and the Antarctic. He follows, therefore, in many ways, in the footsteps of Frank Debenham, the first Director.

Deb was totally convinced of the prime role to be played by SPRI within the University of Cambridge: it was as a memorial for those who had died with Capt. Scott in 1912 on the Antarctic ice-shelf. Quite properly it was called the Scott Polar Research Institute, and the entrance door was surmounted by a bust of Scott, carved by his widow Kathleen. Wilson's finely painted watercolours would be displayed in the Gallery, and the museum would display those artefacts that had been brought back from the Antarctic. If the institute had been built in London, this memorial function might have been enough. The public could visit, and the memories of Scott in the Antarctic would be perpetuated. But SPRI was built in Cambridge, and by grace of the Senate was part of the University. Deb realised that the Institute must fulfil its other role, if at first a secondary one: it must promote research into polar regions, not simply into the physical aspects of ice-covered lands and oceans seasonally covered by ice, but also into those lands in the Arctic that are the traditional homes of peoples skilled in hunting on land and in the adjacent polar seas. In the Antarctic, too, though never inhabited, it was evident, even in 1920, that this southern continent and ocean would become a competitive economic resource for commercial fishing, and possibly for the extraction of minerals. Eventually it would become a region fiercely contested by rival nations on the question of sovereignty. Fortunately, this international dispute was settled, at least temporarily, by the Antarctic Treaty, signed in December 1959 by 12 nations – Argentina, Australia, Belgium, Chile, France, Japan, New Zealand, Norway, Russia, South Africa, the UK, the USA – and made operative from June 1961.

Deb was aware of these potential outcomes, and realised that the Institute's research should be broad-based and cover questions of economic exploitation, political involvement and sovereignty, and in the north, aboriginal cultures as well as the history of exploration and the nature of ice. However, Deb could never completely divorce his interest in discovery from purely scientific enquiry. He saw SPRI as attracting young men to a polar centre which supported adventure towards the lands unknown, in the last frontiers of exploration. In his own words to Hugh Robert Mill, these would be 'real men', fashioned after his young acolytes Gino Watkins and Augustine Courtauld. Deb seems to have regarded Gino as his alter ego, and the nature of his tragic death in Greenland waters led Deb to arrange for a plaque of Gino to be modelled and hung in SPRI.

At this time there was no consideration that 'real women' would be part of any polar expedition, and the British Antarctic Survey did not offer posts to women scientists for stay in Antarctica until the 1970s. The Institute did not sponsor expeditions to Antarctica in the manner of BAS, so consequently the question of promoting women scientists to serve in the Antarctic did not arise. However, many of the M.Phil. and Ph.D. women students who came to the Institute had personal experience of serving at Antarctic bases, particularly at those of the USA. Eventually, in the 1990s, a group primarily of women reading for their Ph.D. carried out research on Cuverville Island, off the Arctowski Peninsula, Antarctic Peninsula, under the supervision of Dr Bernard Stonehouse during successive austral summers.

Coupled with these searches for the unknown at 'the ends of the earth' was the prerequisite for surveying and map-making. There is no evidence that Deb had himself been trained as a surveyor as part of his early academic studies, nor had he considered following surveying as a career. Capt. Scott seemed to think that his scientists would all have some skills in this direction, and Deb was drawn into polar survey and cartography almost accidentally. Presumably he had carried out, under Edgeworth David, some geological mapping in Australia as part of his degree in geology at Sydney University and was, in consequence, familiar with instruments and techniques. At least he carried with him in *Terra Nova* a plane-table and associated instruments, and he demonstrated its utility as an instrument, ideal in those circumstances, for the amateur. Later Deb promoted the plane-table's value to geographers and natural scientists in the Department of Geography at Cambridge, but by this time he had attended a summer course in surveying in Chatham, the home of the Royal Engineer's school of surveying (letter to King, 1921).

Following his retirement in 1946, Deb continued to live close to SPRI at Herne Lodge, St Eligius Street. He persisted in his strong belief that the Institute should attract research workers in both polar hemispheres. This was initially to examine those features that the North and South polar regions had in common, such as the physical nature of ice, the characteristics of cold climates, and the reaction of the human body and mind to extremes of temperature. He accepted, of course, that there were unique features of the Arctic that could have no comparison in the Antarctic because of the long period of habitation of indigenous peoples in the high latitudes of northern lands and the total absence of a settled population in the South. Yet Deb never visited the Arctic countries, which were readily accessible from Cambridge compared to the long journey to Antarctica. Deb found that his life in Cambridge was heavy with administration and organisation, and time consuming with College and University councils, so that an extended tour to the Polar North proved impossible. His Antarctic colleagues, Raymond Priestley, Charles Wright and Griffith Taylor, were similarly afflicted and had no time for further exploration. Cherry-Garrard, who had the time, was periodically too unwell to travel into hostile terrain. It was left to their younger Cambridge associate James Wordie to join undergraduate expeditions to Svalbard and Greenland.

Plans were inaugurated for a second major extension to SPRI's facilities during John Heap's directorship (1992–98). The University agreed a scheme for extending the Library & Information Service by increasing the floor area for readers, providing more shelving, and improving the photography and archive spaces. Additionally a remodelling of the reception area was planned, together with the installation of a lift through four floors, and the building of a study room for postgraduate students. The former map room was to be transferred to the basement and the upper floor would have new offices. The new wing was to be named the Shackleton Memorial Library, after Sir Ernest Shackleton (1874–1922) of *Endurance* fame and his son Lord Edward Shackleton (1911–94), who as an Oxford undergraduate had taken part in an Arctic expedition to Ellesmere Island, in northern Canada, and northern Greenland (1934–35) and had achieved distinction as scientist, conservationist and diplomat. In 1976 he produced *Economic Survey of the Falkland Islands*, and updated the report in 1982 after the Falkland Islands war.

Deb had fondly hoped that room would be found to commemorate Edward Wilson and Birdie Bowers, either in the shape of a lecture theatre, an endowed bursary, or perhaps an annual lecture. By the 1990s time had given a new dimension to the memorial qualities of SPRI, and there was a warm welcome for the proposal to commemorate Sir Ernest Shackleton, another great British polar explorer, to join the pantheon of 'polar greats' (he was actually born in Ireland, but before the Republic was created). Deb's wishes for Wilson and Bowers seemed to have been forgotten.

It was estimated that the total cost of the Shackleton Library would be about £1 million, of which the University would provide £350,000. John Heap was able to approach the many international connections he had made whilst at the Foreign Office, particularly at the numerous Antarctic Treaty meetings where he represented the United Kingdom. Consequently, variable sums from home and overseas sources were attracted to the project, from governments, universities, commerce and private donation. Appropriately, the Government of the British Antarctic Territories, based in Stanley, Falkland Islands, made a contribution. One major gift came, privately, from Tom Manning in Canada. He had been an undergraduate at Cambridge in the 1930s, and a member of the Mountaineering and Explorers' Club, and had subsequently travelled in the Canadian Far North. It was decided to name the new archive section of the Library after him. The Friends of SPRI were also approached for individual contributions, resulting in the collective purchase of the two main library doors with fine glass panels etched with portraits of Ernest and Edward Shackleton.

The building eventually cost £1.25 million, the plans having been prepared by the local firm of John Miller and Partners (architects Richard Brierley and Kristine Ngan). The most striking feature of the extension is the rotunda, which houses on four floors the book shelving and reader spaces. Externally, the materials were chosen to match the original 1934 building – Ketton stone bands alternating with matching stock bricks, with curved glass windows facing the original front of the Institute on Lensfield Road. Internally the floors are linked by a wide spiral staircase.

The Arctic gallery, 1994 (P. Speak)

Deb may not have been too happy with the dedication of the extension, but would have been delighted to see his fine oak block parquet floors repeated, as well as all the oak joinery for panelling and shelving. The Shackleton Memorial Library continues the standards set by Deb, and is regarded as one of the handsomest of Cambridge's many university buildings.

The principal contractor was Haymills, one of the largest firms in southern England. The opportunity was taken to reorganise the reception area on the ground floor, providing new offices, a new kitchen and a lift enclosed in opaque glass to resemble the appearance of glacial ice. Capt. Joe Wubbold, a recent mature M.Phil. student, volunteered to act as project manager for the Institute during the entire building process. In recognition of his invaluable help, the third-floor room, equipped with study carrels for postgraduate students and close shelving for the Institute's unique pamphlet and small brochure collection, has been named 'The Wubbold Room'. The new Library annexe was completed in 1998 and opened by the Hon. Alexandra Shackleton, grand-daughter of Sir Ernest. There is no doubt that the SPRI Library now houses the largest and most comprehensive collection of polar information anywhere in the world.

SPRI, new entrance showing first major extension, 1968 (P. Speak)

The Institute has been fortunate in the appointment of librarians who have held their posts for many years. Harry King was Librarian from 1954 to 1983, assisted by Ann Savours (Shirley) from 1954 to 1970, when she left to join the staff of the National Maritime Museum, Greenwich. She also acted as Archivist, and was replaced by Clive Holland, who produced a large detailed catalogue of manuscripts held in the Library (Holland, 1982). He resigned in 1985 and was replaced by Robert Headland, who had just published *The Island of South Georgia*, representing five years' of research with the British Antarctic Survey, culminating with his early involvement with the Falkland Islands war. Bob resigned his post in 2005, to continue his writings on polar matters and to act as a tourist guide in both the Arctic and the Antarctic. His major published work was completed whilst he was at SPRI, the definitive *Chronological List of Antarctic Expeditions and Related Historical Events* (1989).

Harry King was succeeded by Valerie Galpin for a few years, until the post of Librarian was offered to William Mills (1951–2004). William was enthusiastic for maintaining SPRI's reputation for the excellence of its Library and Information Service, and published books on polar history and polar information retrieval. He

died in 2004 after a long illness, well remembered in SPRI for his strong commitment and fine organisational skills. William was succeeded in November 2004 by the
present Librarian, Heather Lane. It is impossible to evaluate the importance to the
Institute of these and many other members of staff who have been prepared to devote
most of their professional lives to the Institute, for it continues a tradition of high
quality service that was initiated by Frank Debenham.

Another important development that continues today was the inauguration of the
Association of Friends of SPRI, on 27 April 1946, which achieved a membership of
164 in its first year. This was when Deb was considering retirement from the
Directorship of SPRI, and although the aims of the Friends resonated strongly with
Deb's wishes for the future of the Institute, he did not take any official position within
the Association. In its early years, the Committee consisted of James Wordie, Louis
Clarke, Colin Bertram, Vaughan Lewis and Launcelot Fleming, and was drawn from
the staff or the management of the Institute. The Friends pledged to promote the
work of the Institute and to use its fund on behalf of the Institute. Early purchases
were two polar libraries: from Professor Tanner of Sweden and from Professor
Breitfuss of Germany. In a similar manner, the Friends have been able to purchase
items for the Institute and to assist in the purchase of major polar treasures in the
realms of painting, sculpture and books. Whenever extensions to the building were
contemplated, the Friends could be relied upon to make a major contribution. From
its very beginnings the Friends have been responsible for organising Saturday evening
lectures in the Michaelmas and Lent terms, and have continued the tradition of
hosting a summer lunch party.

From the mid-1970s there had been increasing opportunities for tourist travel to
Antarctica and the Southern Ocean, with a consequent increased interest in the polar
regions of the world. By 2007 the Friends had grown to a total membership of over
600, largely due to the inspired successive chairmanships in the 1990s and 2000s of
Philippa Foster Back, OBE, Deb's grand-daughter, David Wilson, a great-nephew of
Edward Wilson who had died with Scott in Antarctica, and Robin Back, Philippa's
brother.

Epilogue

In an obituary appreciation of Frank Debenham published in 1966, a former student of Deb's who had matriculated in 1941 wrote:

> 'At this time I was living in the Debenham household and soon discovered Deb's ability to work all day and night. Creeping into the house in the early hours of the morning, after a dance, I would see the light on in his study and Deb sitting at his table surrounded by reference books and pages of concise notes and diagrams. His mind would be so active, his enthusiasm so infectious, I would forget the lateness of the hour as he developed some new theory in an attempt to answer the problems encountered the previous day.' (Hewitt, 1966: 458)

In the same appreciation another of Deb's former wartime students, Hilda Richardson, who later became the long-serving editor of the *Journal of Glaciology* added:

> 'Deb wrote easily and well on many subjects. He had that rare gift of being able to instruct as well as entertain his reader. He had the facility for lucid explanations of complicated subjects.' (Richardson, 1966; 459)

There are many who have spoken of Deb's academic attributes, not least being his ability to communicate with his students in the lecture room and in the field. He was always approachable even by the youngest of his audiences, especially when the enquiry came from a young child asking about Capt. Scott or the icy wastes of polar regions. Several of his books were written especially for children.

Deb was a prolific writer on a wide variety of topics (see Appendix). He wrote many scientific papers, mainly on glaciology, several instruction manuals, particularly on surveying and navigation, collections of reminiscences of his time on *Terra Nova*, the history of polar exploration, and later in his life travel books of his extensive researches in central Africa. His style is fluid, easy to read, and his material always fascinating whether it is about the poles, the tropics or his contributions to geographical atlases and encyclopedias.

Many colleagues, students and friends have speculated on Deb's omission to produce for publication a personal account of his times with Capt. Scott and the *Terra*

Nova Expedition. All his fellow scientists reproduced their own diaries or contributed to joint accounts of this most famous of polar expeditions, and Deb had to hand the detailed diaries he kept of his time in Antarctica. Apparently Deb considered that there was already a sufficient *Terra Nova* literary collection and anything he might write would appear superfluous. It was not until 1952, after he had retired from full-time work, that he published his own somewhat idiosyncratic account *In the Antarctic: Stories of Scott's Last Expedition.* This little book is dedicated 'To the memory of "Our Bill"', that is, to Edward Adrian Wilson, who died alongside Capt. Scott in the retreat from the Pole'. Deb explained in the foreword, 'When, as a junior member of Scott's Last Expedition I returned in 1913, I resolved not to publish any reminiscences since there were so many others more fitted to do so.' He added that he had now 'broken the vow, in order to deal with the lighter side of those fateful, yet happy three years.' The work is a series of separate accounts of episodes at Cape Evans, mainly inside the hut during the long first winter, when celebratory parties were held, together with general observations on icebergs, and the celebrated 'headless fish'. The illustrations are taken from original sketches by Wilson in the *South Polar Times*, and some by Deb himself. His longer book, *Antarctica: The Story of a Continent*, was not published until 1959 and is essentially a history of the discovery of Antarctica, with only a short chapter on Capt. Scott's two expeditions. Deb's Journals (in reality, his *Diaries*) were transcribed by his daughter June Debenham Back and published for the first time in 1992, together with the illustrations he had drawn whilst in his Antarctic hut, as *The Quiet Land.*

Deb would occasionally come to the Institute and take tea with the staff and occasional visitors. In the summer this would take place on the grass outside the Institute, beneath the two large false acacia trees still standing close to the new entrance. At home Deb wrote short stories, woven imaginatively around these gatherings, and his eldest daughter Barbara had them published in 1997 as *In The Arctic* and *Tales Told at Tea-Time*, nicely illustrated by Deb's drawings. They show Deb's continuing fascination with the Polar North, despite never having been there, even in his retirement, and his fondness for his Institute and its associates. In the Foreword to Barbara's book, Ann Savours expresses the views of those lucky enough to share these occasions:

> 'We loved Deb's kindliness, his gentle leg-pulling, his encouragement and his constant interest in polar people and polar matters, whether of great or lesser import.
>
> We thought of him chiefly as an expert on the Antarctic. These *Tales Told at Tea Time* show that he had a considerable interest in, and knowledge of, the Arctic regions and their history, as befitted the Founding Director of the Polar Institute.'

Ann, whilst working as Assistant Librarian, lodged for some years with the Debenham family at Herne Lodge, and figures in a number of the *Tales*. Others who were regularly present included Terence Armstrong, John Heap, Harry King, Max Forbes (editor pf *Polar Record*) and Charles Swithinbank.

It might have been expected that Deb would have published a major treatise on polar exploration, particularly as he gave several papers to the RGS and to British Association conferences for the Advancement of Science. His only contribution in this specialist field is *The Polar Regions*, published in 1930 as part of the excellent series of popular introductory booklets, Benn's Sixpenny Library. Deb's small book (80 pages) is authoritative and first class as an introduction to the subject and matches well other titles in the same series, also produced by senior members of British universities, but is hardly the substantial and durable volume some had been expecting. Perhaps the most erudite of his academic publications was a work which absorbed him for most of the 1920s and 1930s; this was his editing of a translation from the Russian of *The Voyage of Captain Bellinghausen to the Antarctic Seas, 1819–1821*, published in 1945. This was one of the earliest of all explorations to Antarctica and a prelude to Russia's continuing interest in the continent.

One of Deb's first tasks after his retirement was to act as general editor for a series of introductory texts: *Teach yourself Geography*, published by English Universities Press. Deb produced the first volume in 1950: 'The use of geography', and persuaded his colleagues in the Cambridge Department of Geography to write the others: 'Economic geography', 'Historical geography', 'Biogeography' and 'Physical geography'.

Unfortunately this was just the time when the subject was under close scrutiny and new ideas were being advanced. It resulted in the books having a very short shelf-life as they were soon overtaken by less descriptive, loftier and more penetrating volumes. However, it is instructive to read what Deb, at this time, considered to be the central themes of geography. He defines geography as the 'philosophy of place' and believes that 'We are all geographers in some degree, and we can fit ourselves to join in the research for wisdom with respect to Place, in the hope of arriving at some measure of understanding' (*The Use of Geography*, 1950). He repeats a remark attributed to Sir Halford Mackinder of Oxford at the start of the century that 'Geography is a point of view', a somewhat ambiguous definition and one that gave rise to much criticism from many of the subject's companion disciplines. The chapter headings of Deb's book indicate that his traditional view of the substance of geography was changing and new brooms were beginning to sweep: The philosophy of place, The history of geography, Geography from the arm-chair, Geography in the field, Human geography, World food production, The price of a cow, and so on. Few would disagree still, however, with Deb's emphasis on physical geography as the basis of the discipline, but whilst endorsing its subject matter as eclectic, would not agree it as an omnium gatherum. Deb firmly believed that 'the Geographer puts Place as his background, instead of Number or Abstract Concept.' He also urged the reader to 'Travel as widely as you can.'

Deb was also a very practical man, whether he was teaching in the lecture room or in the field. His courses in surveying influenced countless students, who were required to map in the field be it water courses, archaeological sites or plant distribu-tions; they were essentially for the natural scientist rather than for the professional surveyor. Deb expected that the scientist would also have the cartographic skills of map preparation in the techniques of applying colour washes, scale lines and relief repre-sentation. He experimented himself in the techniques of vertical and oblique hill shading for the portrayal of relief features, both on topographic and atlas maps. In his extensive travels across central Africa in the 1950s, he mapped his journeys by compass traverse and triangulation, with comparative heights measured by aneroid barometer and with hand-drawing of the rivers flowing into the Benguela Swamps and the arid features of the Kalahari desert. Place names and topographic features were added by hand, and the maps published in his travel writings and scientific reports. He used his experiences on these expeditions to write two major works on Africa, *The Way to Ilala* (1955), essentially an account of the 'Pilgrimage of David Livingstone', and *Kalahari Sand* (1953). It was as though in retirement he was recalling the exploring and mapping he did as a young man with Capt. Scott, but in a very different terrain.

Deb's writings are enlivened by numerous quotations, from Bunyan's *Pilgrim's Progress*, from Shakespeare, and particularly from *Alice in Wonderland*. Some of his lighter writings were especially for children.

He was also a pioneer in the construction of laboratory equipment for the simu-lation of stream and wave action as a teaching aid to the understanding of natural processes. His hydrological laboratory became a model for similar labs to be built in other departments of geography. W. W. Williams, former lecturer, has recalled that the equipment was used to simulate the conditions expected during the Normandy land-ings on D-Day.

In Cambridge he has two great memorial buildings, the Department of Geography and the Scott Polar Research Institute. Both reflect Deb's intentions to create beautiful buildings that would grace the University and provide centres for specialised research. The buildings contain well-proportioned rooms with adjacent libraries, laboratories and lecture theatres. They engender a feeling of warm fellow-ship in a common aim amongst those using the buildings. Amongst the splendid surroundings of objets d'art, the sociability and the atmosphere of an academic special club has been fostered. Deb was careful to decorate the interiors with murals, photo-graphs and maps, for adornment as much as for instruction. At SPRI he was able to exhibit polar equipment from historical expeditions, and to augment them with sculptures and other works of art, loaned, given or bought from varied polar places. Thus SPRI has a priceless collection of scrimshaw (ivory and bone carvings) and traditional indigenous clothing from widely scattered Arctic peoples such as the North American Eskimos and Inuit, the Sami of Scandinavia, and the reindeer herders of Siberia.

All this work involved Deb with interminable negotiation with the Senate of the University, with fund-awarding bodies such as the Royal Society and the RGS, as well as with architects, builders and interior decorators. Hugh Robert Mill has described Deb as 'a natural diplomat who accepts a rebuff with a smile, but the smile usually turned aside any risk of failure' (Mill, 1947: 5). He certainly seems to have prosecuted his planning with great vigour and an attitude of extreme friendliness. Only in this way was he able to move from an unfurnished attic room in the Sedgwick Building to the beautiful house and garden of Lensfield House, and to oversee the construction of the present handsome building of SPRI, whilst persisting with the Department of Geography until new premises were built on the Downing site. At no time is there any indication in his personal papers that he ever contemplated moving away from Cambridge after 1913 for a post where life might have been easier.

From the middle of the 1950s Deb suffered increasing bouts of ill health, but enjoyed a very happy home life with his large family and sheltered by Dorothy from the strains of too much work.

Deb's last visit back to Australia was in 1959 as observer at the Third Meeting of the Scientific Committee on Antarctic Research held in Canberra. His compatriot, Gordon Robin, a new Director of the Institute, was the official delegate from the United Kingdom. On returning to Cambridge, Deb's failing health became apparent. He wrote on 15 June 1959 to Ann Shirley (Savours):

> 'My Dear Ann,
> I am not allowed out of my room for a week or two. I have finished two small books – Simple Surveying for Australian Farmers, and Navigation with Alice. I saw J. K. Davis [Captain in Antarctica of Shackleton's *Nimrod* and Mawson's *Aurora*] in Melbourne. Adelaide University are thinking of a memorial to Douglas Mawson on lines of SPRI.'
>
> (A. Savours, personal communication)

On the way back via North America he stopped to see Charles Wright in Vancouver and Beryl Bird at the Arctic Institute of Canada. He admitted to attempting too much in Australia – lectures, broadcasting and conferences. He was pleased to see that Gordon Robin had gone down well at the Conference, supported by Deb and Raymond Priestley, but added: 'After being a minnow in the Cambridge pond I was rather taken aback at finding myself a whale in the Australian pond!'

Deb had come a long way from his early days in Bowral, New South Wales. The wheel of good fortune had turned favourably in his direction when he decided to return to the University of Sydney to read for a degree in geology in 1908, where he met Professor Edgeworth David who recommended him to Capt. Scott for the *Terra Nova* Expedition. The rest of his life followed from these fortuitous encounters: Antarctica, a fellowship of polar scientists whom he joined on their return to Cambridge; an embryonic Department of Geography looking for a physical scientist with survey experience; and the chance to prepare a polar research centre as a memorial to those comrades who had perished on the return from attaining the South Pole.

There is a tide in the affairs of men
Which, taken on the flood, leads on to fortune.
Omitted, all the voyage of their life
Is bound in shallows and in miseries.
On such a full sea are we now afloat
And we must take the current when it serves
Or lose our ventures.

                          (Shakespeare, *Julius Caesar*)

Appendix: Publications of Frank Debenham

(1910) Notes on the geology of King Island, *Journal and Proceedings of the Royal Society of New South Wales*, 44, 560–76.

(1913) The geological expedition to Granite Harbour, in *Scott's Last Expedition, Journals of Captain Scott, arranged by Leonard Huxley*,Vol. III. London: Smith Elder, pp. 290, 438–40.

(1914) The Southern Pole: a fragment, *The Caian*, 23, 182–4.

(1915) Notes following a paper by R.F. Scott, The Great Ice Barrier and the inland ice. From the manuscript of a lecture delivered at Cape Evans, June 1911, *Geographical Journal*, 46, 436–46, notes by F. Debenham, 446–7.

(1919) A new theory of transportation by ice: the raised marine muds of South Victoria Land (Antarctica), *Abstracts of Proceedings of the Geological Society of London*, 1041, 93–8.

(1919) A new theory of transportation by ice: the raised marine muds of South Victoria Land (Antarctica), *Journal of the Geological Society*, 75, 51–73, discussion, 73–6.

(1920) Abstract, *Geographical Journal*, 56 (1920), 422.

(1921) The future of polar exploration, *Geographical Journal*, 57, 182–200, discussion, 200–204.

(1921) Antarctic exploration in the future, *Discovery*, 2, 112–17.

(1921) Recent and local deposits of McMurdo Sound region, British Antarctic (*Terra Nova*) Expedition, 1910, *Natural History Report: Geology*, 1(3), 63–100.

(1921) The sandstone, etc., of the McMurdo Sound, Terra Nova Bay, and Beardmore Glacier regions, in *The Sedimentary Rocks of South Victoria Land*, F. Debenham, R.H. Rastall and R.E. Priestley, British Antarctic (*Terra Nova*) Expedition, 1910, *Natural History Report Geology*, 1(4), 103–119.

(1921) The metamorphic rocks of the McMurdo Sound region, W. Campbell Smith and F. Debenham, in *The Metamorphic Rocks of South Victoria Land*, W. Campbell Smith, F. Debenham and R.E. Priestly, British Antarctic (*Terra Nova*) Expedition, 1910, *Natural History Report: Geology*, 1(5), 133–44.

(1923) The physiography of the Ross Archipelago, *British (Terra Nova) Antarctic Expedition 1910–1913*. London: Harrison, pp. i–viii, 1–94.

(1923) *Report on the Maps and Survey of the British (Terra Nova) Antarctic Expedition, 1910–1913*. London: Harrison.

(1926) The Captain Scott Polar Research Institute, *Geographical Journal*, 68, 43–8.

(1928) The Fenlands, in *Great Britain, Essays in Regional Geography*, A.G. Ogivie (ed.). Cambridge: Cambridge University Press, ix, 174–83 (3rd edition published 1952).

(1928) *Structure and Surface: A book of field geology*, C. Barrington Brown and F. Debenham. London: Edward Arnold, i–vii, 1–168.

(1928) Farther afield in exploration, *Discovery*, 10, 187–90.

(1930) Problems of the South Africa sector of Antarctica, Report of the 97th (99th year) British Association for the Advancement of Science, South Africa 1929, 348–9.

(1930) *The Polar Regions*. London: Ernest Benn (Benn's Sixpenny Library), no 150, 1–80.

(1930) Icebergs larger than the Isle of Man, *Discovery*, 11, 90–93.

(1930) Biography of Captain Scott (review of S. Gwynne's Captain Scott), *Geographical Journal*, 75, 357–9.

(1932) International polar research, *Discovery,* 13, 14–16.

(1933) Names on the Antarctic continent, *Geographical Journal,* 81, 145–8.

(1933) The Scott Polar Research Institute, Cambridge, England, its history and aims, *Arctica* (Leningrad), 1, 67–74 (in English, Russian summary).

(1934) The Eskimo kayak, *Polar Record,* 1(7), 5–62.

(1934) An Eskimo kayak voyage to Aberdeen. Report of the Annual Meeting, 1934, British Association for the Advancement of Science, 333.

(1935) Some aspects of the Polar regions. Presidential address to Section E, Report of the Annual Meeting, 1935, British Association for the Advancement of Science, 79–88.

(1935) Polar research. Presidential address to Section E (abstract), *Nature,* 136, 382–3.

(1935) Some aspects of the Polar regions, *Nature,* 136, 459–62.

(1935) Some aspects of the Polar regions, *Scottish Geographical Magazine,* 52, 273–84.

(1936) Exploration by air in the Antarctic, *Journal of the Tyneside Geographical Society,* N.S. 1, 14–17.

(1936) Cheaper plane tables, *Geography,* 21, 222–4.

(1936) *Map Making,* London and Glasgow: Blackie, i–vi, 1–240 (3rd edn published 1955).

(1937) *Exercises in Cartography.* London and Glasgow: Blackie, i–vii, 1–136.

(1939) Tom Crean: an appreciation, *Polar Record,* 3, 778–9.

(1939) Postscipt to paper by G.C.L. Bertram.The use of fuel in polar sledge travel, *Polar Record,* 3(17), 71–5, comment, 74–5.

(1941) Bering's last voyage, *Polar Record,* 3, 421–6.

(1942) The Erebus and Terror at Hobart, *Polar Record,* 3, 468–75.

(1942) Place names in the Polar regions, *Polar Record, 4, 19–24.*

(1942) A laboratory for physical geography, *Geographical Journal,* 3, 541–2.

(1942) *Astrographics, or First Steps in Navigation by the Stars: A primer for the Airman Cadet.* Cambridge: Heffer, 1–118 (2nd edn published 1942).

(1943) Friction on sledge runners (Friction on snow surfaces, Part II), *Polar Record,* 4, 7–11.

(1943) Stareek: the story of a sledge dog, *Polar Record,* 4, 19–20.

(1943) Antarctic regions, *Encyclopaedia Britannica,* 2, 14–20.

(1944) Albert Borlase Armitage – an appreciation (Obituary*), Polar Record,* 4, 186–7.

(1945) Retrospect: the Scott Polar Research Institute, 1920–45, *Polar Record,* 4, 223–35.

(1945) *The voyage of Captain Bellinghausen to the Antarctic Seas, 1819–1821,* translated from the Russian, F. Debenham (ed.). London: Hakluyt Society, Second Series, 91–2, i–xxx, 1-260, 1-216.

(1946) Reports on scientific results of the United States Antarctic Service Expedition, 1939–1941: a review, *Geographical Review,* 36, 483–5.

(1946) *Report on the Navigation Possibilities of the Upper Zambesi,* Lusaka: Government Printer, 1-9.

(1946) *Report on the Bangweula Swamps.* Lusaka: Government Printer, 1–18.

(1947) Lady Kennet: an appreciation, *Polar Record,* 5, 147.

(1947) Scott of the Antarctic, a personal opinion, *Polar Record,* 5, 311–16.

(1947) Nine nations will voyage to discover nothing? *Sunday Express,* 5 January.

(1947) The Bengweula Swamps of Central Africa, *Geographical Review,* 37, 351–68.

(1947) Mill, H.R. (Obituary), *Polar Record,* 3 (33), 5.

(1948) The water resources of Central Africa, *Geographical Journal,* 111, 222–33, discussion, 233–4.

(1948) *Report on the Water Resources of the Bechuanaland Protectorate, Northern Rhodesia, the Nyasaland Protectorate, Tangankika Territory, Kenya and the Uganda Protectorate.* London: His Majesty's Stationery Office, Colonial Research Publication No 2, 1–85.

(1948) *Notes for Water Reconnaissance*. Lusaka: Government Printer, 1–39.

(1948) The problem of the Great Ross Barrier, *Geographical Journal*, 112, 197–212, discussion, 213–18.

(1948) Commander Rupert Gould, R.N. (Obituary), *Geographical Journal*, 112, 258–9.

(1950) *The Use of Geography*. London: English Universities Press, i-x, 1–206 (introductory volume in the series *Teach Yourself Geography*).

(1950) Surveying Bangweula, *Corona*, 2, 215–17.

(1951) River development in Northern Rhodesia, *Corona*, 3, 224–6.

(1951) The changing physical environment of tropical Africa, *Corona*, 3, 367–73.

(1951) Livingstone's Africa and future development, *Geography*, 36, 107–111.

(1951) Development in Bechuanaland, based on his address to the Annual Meeting of the Society on 12 July 1951, *The Anti-Slavery Society*, 1–8.

(1951) Journey in Thirstland: in search of water in Bechuanaland, *Geographical Review*, 41, 464–9.

(1952) The water problems of Africa, *Journal of the Royal Society of Arts*, 100, 147–58.

(1952) The Kalahari today, *Geographical Journal*, 118, 12–21, discussion, 22–3.

(1952) *In the Antarctic: Stories of Scott's last expedition*, with illustrations by Edward Wilson and the author. London: John Murray, i-vii, 1–146.

(1952) *A Pictorial Survey of England and Wales: 2*, East Anglia. London: George Philip, 1–16.

(1952) *Study of an African swamp. Report of the Cambridge University Expedition to the Bangweula Swamps, Northern Rhodesia, 1949*. London: His Majesty's Stationery Office, for the Government of Northern Rhodesia, 1–88.

(1953) 'Travel', Presidential address to the Geographical Association, *Geography*, 38, 117–24.

(1953) Diamond Jubilee Address, Diamond Jubilee Celebration, Sheffield, 26 September 1953, *Geography*, 38, 212–20.

(1953) The study of Lake Nyasa, (letter), *Geographical Journal*, 119, 254–5.

(1953) *Kalahari Sand*. London: Bell.

(1954) New light on Livingstone's last journey, *Geographical Journal*, 120, 1–12, discussion, 12–14.

(1954) Study of Lake Nyasa, *Geographical Journal*, 120–262.

(1954) The geography of deserts, in J.L. Cloudsley-Thompson (ed.) *Biology of Deserts*. London: Institute of Biology.

(1954) *The Proceedings of a Symposium on the Biology of Hot and Cold Deserts, Organised by the Institute of Biology*. London: Instititue of Biology, 1–6.

(1954) The water resources of Africa, *Sudan Notes and Records*, 35(2), 69–75.

(1954) The ice islands of the Arctic: a hypothesis, *Geographical Review*, 44, 495–507.

(1955) Glacierization, (letter), *Journal of Glaciology*, 2, 507.

(1955) David Livingstone and the Zambesi, *Geographical Magazine*, 28, 311–19.

(1955) *The Way to Ilala*. London: Longmans Green, 1–336.

(1955) One hundred years ago: the discovery of the Victoria Falls, in *The Life and Work of David Livingstone*, Guide to the Exhibition, 1 June to 31 August 1955. Livingstone: Rhodes-Livingstone Museum, 9–18.

(1955) *Nyasaland, The Land of the Lake*. London: Her Majesty's Stationery Office, Cororna Library, i-xi, 1–239.

(1956) Surgeon Commander George Murray Levick (RN retired) (Obituary), *Polar Record*, 8, 279.

(1957) Commander John Hugh Mather (Obituary), *Polar Record*, 8, 562.

(1957) *Seven Centuries of Debenhams*. Glasgow: privately printed by Robert MacLehose, 1–64.

(1958) Sir Douglas Mawson, O.B.E., F.R.S. (Obituary), *Geographical Journal*, 124, 584–5.

(1958) *The World is Round: The story of man and maps,* introduction by Bernard Russell. London: MacDonald, in association with Rathbone Books, 1–97.

(1959) *Antarctica: The story of a continent.* London: Herbert Jenkins, 1–264.

(1959) *Antarktis: Geschicte eines Kontinents.* Munchen: Copress-Verlag, 1–232.

(1959) *Gran Bretana en el mundo moderno, La expedition de los desiertos de arena y de la regions polares.* Madrid: Boletin de la Real Sociedad Geografica, 95, 325–9.

(1960) Apsley Cherry-Garrard (Obituary), *Polar Record,* 10, 93.

(1960) Focus on Nyasaland, *Geographical Magazine,* 33, 53–60.

(1960) *Discovery and Exploration: an atlas-history of man's journeys into the unknown.* London: Paul Hamlyn, 1–222.

(1960) *The McGraw-Hill Illustrated World Geography,* F. Debenham with W.A. Burns. New York, Toronto and London: McGraw-Hill, i–xvi, 1–519.

(1964) A simple water level, for the measurement of relative heights and contouring, *Geographical Journal,* 130 (4), 528–30.

(1964) and G. Taylor, Report on Geology British Antarctic, Terra Nova Expedition 1910. *Natural History Reports, Geology,* Vols I and II. London: British Museum.

(1965) The genesis of the McMurdo Ice Shelf, Antarctica, *Journal of Glaciology,* 5, 42, 829–32.

(1997) *In The Arctic* and *Tales Told At Tea-time,* Barbara Debenham (ed.). Banham: Erskine Press, Banham.

Compiled from the Bibliography in *Quietland,* reproduced by D. W.H. Walton from an original by D.R. Stoddart (1966, MS in SPRI, 92-Debenham F), *The Diaries of Frank Debenham,* June Debenham Back, Bluntisham Books, Erskine Press, 1992.

Bibliography

From the Archives of the Scott Polar Research Institute

Incomplete Narrative of the British Antarctic (Terra Nova) Expedition, 1910–1913, to 6 December 1910 (14p) (MS 280/18)

Frank Debenham (1883–1965)

MS 279 (1–4): Journals
  Vol. 1 – 26 November 1910 to 18 January 1911
  Vol. 2 – 19 January to 8 March 1911
  Vol. 3 – 14 April to 1 November 1911 and 1 March to 25 November 1912
  Vol. 4 – 3–26 December 1912 (Mt. Erebus to Cape Royds)
MS 1069: Diary, 1–27 January 1913
MS 100/23/1-78: Letters to Hugh Robert Mill, 1920–47
MS 873/2/7-17: Letters to Apsley Cherry-Garrard, 21 March – 17 July 1920
MS 559/57/1-10: Letters to Apsley Cherry-Garrard, 1916–20

Robert Birley Brian Roberts (1912–78)

* MS 1308/37: Correspondence and papers, 1930–64
* Correspondence with University Financial Board on the foundation of the Scott Polar Research Institute (1920–26)
* Correspondence with Buildings Syndicate of the University on the site for a new building (1929–32)
* Plans for Scott Polar Research Institute building (1933–34)

* These MSS are presently classified. Application to view should be addressed to the Director of the Institute.

General Catalogues

Manuscripts in the Scott Polar Research Institute, Cambridge, England.
A Catalogue (1982) Clive Holland (ed.). New York and London: Garland.
Supplementary catalogue, Scott Polar Research Institute, (from 1982), Naomi Boneham, unpublished, August 2004.

The Royal Geographical Society

F. Debenham (1921) Letter to Col. King, 16 August, RGS, Correspondence, COR-CB9, 1921-30
F. Debenham (1929) Memorandum on Geography at Cambridge University, 10 January, RGS, CB9-1921-1930
Frank Debenham Correspondence 1911–20, 1921–30, 1931–40
Frank Debenham Sketches and Figures, LMS D5

Other Publications

Armstrong, Terrence (1952) *The Northern Sea Route*. Cambridge: SPRI.

Armstrong, Terrence, Graham Rowley and George Rogers (1978) *The Circumpolar North*. London: Methuen.

British Antarctic Survey (BAS) (1991) *The History of Place-names in the British Antarctic Territory*, G. Hattersley-Smith (ed.), Scientific Reports No. 113, Part I. Cambridge: BAS.

Bryan, Peter and Nick Wise (2005) Cambridge New town – A Victorian Microcosm. Proceedings of the Cambridge Antiquarian Society, Alison Taylor (ed.), XCIV, 205, 199–216.

Cambridge University Reporter (1918–19) 274, 432.

Cherry-Garrard, Apsley (1922) *The Worst Journey in the World*. London: Penguin.

Debenham Back, June (ed.) (1992) *The Quiet Land: The Antarctic Diaries of Frank Debenham*. Huntingdon: Erskine Press/Bluntisham Books.

Drewry, David J. (ed.) (1983) *Antarctica: Glaciological and Geological Folio*. Cambridge: Scott Polar Research Institute.

Fiennes, Rannulph (2003) *Captain Scott*. London: Hodder and Stoughton.

Fuchs, Vivian (1992) *Of Ice and Men*. Oswestry: Antony Nelson.

Headland, Robert (1984) *The Island of South Georgia*. Cambridge: Cambridge University Press.

Headland, Robert (1989) *Chronological List of Antarctic Expeditions and Related Historical Events*. Cambridge: Cambridge University Press.

Hewitt, Shirley (1966) Frank Debenham (Obituary), *Journal of Glaciology*, 6. 45, 455–9.

Hinks, A.R. (1913) *Maps and Survey*. Cambridge: Cambridge University Press.

Holland, C. (1982) *Manuscripts in the SPRI, Cambridge, England: A Catalogue*. New York: Garland.

Hudson, Doctor (1965) *Daily Telegraph*, 2 September (SPRI folder 92 Debenham F).

Jones, Max (ed.) (2005) *Robert Falcon Scott Journals, Scott's Last Expedition*. Oxford: Oxford University Press.

Kapitsa, Andrey P., Jeffery K. Ridley, Gordon de Quettville Robin, Martin J. Siegert and Igor A. Zotikov (1996) A large, deep freshwater lake beneath the ice of central east Antarctica, *Nature*, 381 (20 June) 684–6.

Keltie, John Scott (1986) Report to the Council of the Royal Geographical Society of geographical education, *Supplementary Papers of the Royal Geographical Society*, 1 (4), 439–554.

Kennet, Kathleen (1949) *Self Portrait of an Artist: From the diaries and memories of Lady Kennet, Kathleen, Lady Scott*. London: John Murray.

King, H.G.R. (1980) Polar studies in Cambridge, *The Magazine of the Cambridge Society*, 7, 38–45.

King, H.G.R. and Ann Savours (eds) (1995) *Polar Pundit: Reminiscences of Brian Birley Roberts*. Cambridge: SPRI. p. 111.

Lake, Philip (1915/1958) *Physical Geography*, 4th edn, J.A. Steers (ed.). Cambridge: Cambridge University Press.

Mackinder, H.J. (1887) *On the Scope and Methods of Geography*, Proceedings of the Royal Geographical Society, n.s. 9, 141–60.

Manley, G. (1966) Frank Debenham (Obituary), *Journal of Glaciology*, 6, 456–7.

Mill, H.R. (1905) *The Siege of the South Pole: The Story of Antarctic Exploration*. London: Alston Rivers.

Mill, H.R. (1907) *The Realm of Nature: An Outline of Physiography*. London: John Murray.

Polar Record (1935) Opening Ceremony and Description of New Building, 9, 2–9.

Pound, Reginald (1968) *Scott of the Antarctic*. London: World Books, p. 221.

Roberts, Brian (ed.) (1967) *Edward Wilson's Birds of Antarctica*. London: Blandford (revised 1980).

Roberts, Brian with T.E. Armstrong and C.W.M. Swithinbank (1966) *Illustrated Glossary of Snow and Ice*. Cambridge: SPRI.

Robin, Gordon de Q. (1966) Frank Debenham (Obituary), *Polar Record*, 13, 82, 215–17.

Shackleton, Lord E. (1982) *Economic Survey of the Falkland Islands*. London: HMSO.

Smith, Michael (2001) *An Unsung Hero: Tom Crean – Antarctic Survivor*. London: Headline.

Smith, Michael (2002) '*I Am Just Going Outside*', *Captain Oates – Antarctic Tragedy*. Staplehurst: Spellmount.

Smith, Michael (2004) *Sir James Wordie, Polar Crusader*. Edinburgh: Birlinn.

Steers, J.A. (ed.) (1934) *Scolt Head Island*. Cambridge: Heffer (revised 1960).

Steers, J.A. (1966) Frank Debenham (Obituary), *Geographical Journal*, 132, 173–5.

Stoddart, Dr David Ross (1975) The RGS and the foundations of geography at Cambridge, *Geographical Journal*, 141, 216–40.

Stoddart, Dr David Ross (1986) *On Geography*. Oxford: Blackwell, Chapters 4, 5 and 9.

Stonehouse, Bernard (1981) Trygve Gran (Obituary), *Polar Record*, 20, 180.

Taylor, Griffith (1977) *The Terra Nova Expedition*. Banham: Bluntisham Books, p. 453–4.

University Reporter (1965) 4466, XCV, 48, 2087.

Wheeler, Sara (2001) *Cherry: A Life of Apsley Cherry-Garrard*. London: Jonathan Cape.

Wilson, D.M. and D.B. Elder (2000) *Cheltenham in Antarctica: The Life of Edward Wilson*. Cheltenham: Reardon.

Wright, Charles (1975) Raymond Priestley (Obituary), *Polar Record*, 17, 215.

Index

The Friends of the Scott Polar Research Institute

The association of Friends was established in 1946 to provide individuals with a way of supporting the important work of the Institute. Funds are raised through subscriptions of varying levels to suit all pockets. The Friends provide assistance to all aspects of the Institute's work as requested by Institute staff, principally through financial and practical help for the Library, Museum and Picture Library.

Ways in which the Friends give ongoing support include:

• providing materials for museum exhibits
• supporting conservation work on the photographic collections
• providing for the essential repair of books
• purchasing maps and out-of-print publications
• assisting in the preservation of the Picture Library's film footage
• providing grants to support the work of polar specialists
• assisting in the acquisition of archivally important journals and letters
• holding special appeals to enable extra support for the Institute
• contributions towards the cost of restoring historic artefacts.

Practical help by volunteer Friends has included working on the map collection, documentation and storage of the museum collection, photographic cataloguing, scanning newspaper articles.

News and information about the Institute and other polar activities is circulated to members through their newsletter. As well as arranging the popular Saturday evening public lecture series, the Friends regularly hold social events, giving individuals the opportunity to meet other Friends and members of the Institute.

Anyone wishing to join the Friends and help continue the valuable work of the Scott Polar Research Institute should either e-mail friends@spri.cam.ac.uk or Tel: +44 (0)1223 336540.